Animal Prayer Guide

A Book Based On ... ...pture

Niki Behrikis Shanahan

Author Of

There Is Eternal Life For Animals

Published By:

Pete Publishing
Tyngsborough, Massachusetts

We Welcome You To Visit Us At:

http://www.eternalanimals.com

Animal Prayer Guide

First Published 2005
Printed and bound in the United States of America

ISBN-10: 0972030123
ISBN-13: 978-0972030123
Library of Congress Control Number: 2005900311

Published By:

Pete Publishing
P. O. Box 282
Tyngsborough, MA 01879

http://www.eternalanimals.com

Cover Photography of Cat (Luke) and Horse
Copyright 2005, Niki Behrikis Shanahan

Cover Photography of Sheltie Dog, Lena
Copyright 2005, Janis Nedelec

(Cat on cover is author's animal companion, Luke Shanahan)

Acknowledgments

I wish to thank the following people for their assistance in making the book *Animal Prayer Guide* possible:

Jesus Christ, our Lord and Savior, who made the salvation, healing, and help for mankind and animals possible. If this book is helpful and beneficial to anyone, it is due to the guidance and knowledge given to me by the Good Shepherd.

My husband, Jack, Editor, for his excellent detail-oriented contributions and valuable suggestions to make this book possible. He provides all our vital Technical Support that make our publications and website possible. This includes manuscript layout, e-book conversions, inventory spreadsheets, and every aspect of day-to-day computer maintenance. He is a committed Prayer Partner for all our website prayer requests that we receive, has a real heart for all animals and a strong love for the Lord. He assists with fulfilling our orders, and is a great help in keeping me organized. I rely on him as a consultant on a daily basis. Jack is a significant part of this ministry, and a great blessing to me.

Janis Nedelec, Editor, for all her hard and efficient work reviewing this manuscript. She has had many excellent suggestions to share, and spent a considerable amount of time reviewing this book. Janis is an invaluable contributor to this ministry! From British Columbia, Canada, Janis is a dedicated Prayer Partner for all requests that are received from our website. Janis regularly contributes information, stories, and photos for our website. She donates her time to contact magazines, newspapers, publications, pet loss counselors, veterinarians, churches, and pet sites to let them know about our website and our first book, *There Is Eternal Life For Animals*. Her great love for animals and the Lord come through strongly each and every day. Janis has been a great friend and blessing to me personally, and I praise God for bringing us together.

Dedication

I dedicate this book to my three cats, Pete, Lukie, Joey, and all the animals of the world. Pete was my first pet, and he is most responsible for the great love I have for animals. I adopted Pete when he was 8 years old and he lived to be over 21 years of age. He belonged to someone in the condominium building where we lived, and that person no longer wanted him. Guess what – we did! Pete was and still is the love of my life. Pete is now in heaven and quite alive and well. He is patiently waiting for our arrival so he can be with his whole family again for eternity! I was only able to contribute *There Is Eternal Life For Animals,* which proves scripturally that all animals go to heaven, because of my tremendous love for Pete.

Lukie was one of several feral cats that I used to feed on a daily basis. He was six months old when I went out to feed him one day determined that I was going to catch him. I wasn't experienced in using traps at all, and with a lot of praying, I decided to go out with some tuna fish and wave it around in front of Lukie. Thanks to the Lord, Lukie came close enough for me to grab him and with my car door open, my pet carrier door open, which was on the back seat, I put him in the carrier as fast as I could. He quickly became part of our family, and he and Pete loved each other immediately. Lukie is a real sweet boy and a joy to be with every day.

Joey became part of the family right after Pete left. There have been very few cats running around in our neighborhood we now live in, and he was a stray that we adopted. We began to give him food and water whenever he came by in an area in our backyard. Then one day I told him that he could go up on the deck if he wanted to, and didn't have to stay and eat in the back of the yard. The very next day he was up on the deck! Animals are so smart, aren't they? We started bringing him in our basement when it was snowing and very cold outside, and eventually adopted him.

We leave sunflower seeds outside for all the birds, chipmunks, squirrels and whoever shows up. Lukie and Joey love watching their little friends eating outside. We've even involuntarily donated our huge Blue Angel hosta plant to the deer a couple of years in a row! They love eating the huge leaves of this hosta plant. We love all animals, pray for them everyday, and hope that you will, too.

Preface

After I wrote the book *There Is Eternal Life For Animals,* I created a website. I decided that we would like to take prayer requests for any sick animals, lost pets, and animals with any kind of need. I was amazed at how many people requested prayer for their animal companions. I also joined other pet prayer groups and began praying with them. Soon I realized that animals and their pet parents had many needs, and I felt that a book dedicated to praying for animals would be a great blessing to them all. Also, there are too many animals that have no representatives to protect and speak up for them. We want to pray for all their needs, including food, water, shelter, and protection from anyone or anything that would harm them. I pray that this book blesses many, many animals, pet parents, and those who are dedicated to helping them.

Foreword

Animal Prayer Guide is a wonderfully comforting and inspirational book!

By writing *Animal Prayer Guide*, Niki Behrikis Shanahan has empowered the laity to pray and hold services for their beloved animal companions and for all other animals. Unfortunately, this is something that most clergy have refused or have been very reluctant to do.

For many people, companion animals are like their children. They want them to be healthy and happy and to enjoy the life God has given them. They're concerned when they're sick, and they mourn deeply over their loss. As a retired pastor, I continue to counsel and pray with people who grieve over the death of any loved one, and it is obvious that the emotional stress is the same for both humans and other animals. These people want the assurance that beloved companions will be in heaven. *Animal Prayer Guide* will make this comforting ministry easier.

Throughout this book the author has shown the world that all living beings, whether human or non-human, were lovingly created by God, and that there is a place in heaven for us all. Furthermore, this book confirms that all beings are worthy of our prayers and God's blessings. If it is proper to pray for humans, it is also proper to pray for all other animals.

Sample blessings and prayers are sprinkled throughout all the chapters of *Animal Prayer Guide*, and in the last chapter there is a sample memorial service.

Niki Behrikis Shanahan's *Animal Prayer Guide* is a much needed "tool" to help people comfortably pray for animals, everywhere and for every need. Thank you, Niki, for writing it.

Frank L. Hoffman
The Mary T. and Frank L. Hoffman Family Foundation
Athens, New York, www.all-creatures.org

"Absolutely packed full of essential knowledge, this work should be kept as a reference book for all those who love God's creation. It is clear and concise, informative and Biblical, yet folded within the pages is the heart of God, His love for you and His love for His creation. This is a must read, a must have reference work, that you will refer to time and time again. Questions answered and backed-up by Scripture, sample prayers to help you along the way, and encouragement to never give up can all be found within the pages of this book."

Rev. Shirley Johnson, Florida
Senior Reviewer, MidWest Book Review

"Animal Prayer Guide is a lifelong treasury of hope and love not only for you and your cherished companion animals, but also for all of those less fortunate who are lost, alone and abandoned. Based purely on Bible Scripture, the prayers in *Animal Prayer Guide* will be a source of comfort and assurance for you and your pets for many years to come. Filled with numerous true stories of wit and wisdom in equal parts, Ms. Shanahan's second book is a pure delight. This book shatters the myth that animals are outside the circle of God's abiding love and compassion, and calls upon all of us to be Good Shepherds ... not only for our own pets, but for ALL of God's creatures."

Annie Mals
President, The Peaceful Kingdom
Alliance 4 Animals, California

"I just finished reading *Animal Prayer Guide*, and it is a beautiful book! You have not only told how to properly pray for our pets and all animals, you have also provided a good start for anyone who wants to learn how to pray in faith and get results. The stories you included were heartwarming and special, and you have included much Scripture as a basis for all that you are sharing. This book will be a blessing to animal lovers, just as *There Is Eternal Life For Animals* has been."

Frances Weber
President & Founder, The Ark
South Carolina

"There has long been a need for such a prayer guide and I am very grateful to the Lord that He has inspired Niki Behrikis Shanahan to produce this labor of love. The *Animal Prayer Guide* is a logical and worthy sequel to her book *There Is Eternal Life For Animals*. It will be an encouragement, inspiration, and comfort to many of God's people who love God's animals."

Rev. Dr. Peter Hammond
Founder and Director of Frontline Fellowship
Cape Town, South Africa

"My prescription: provide good food and exercise, see your veterinarian for yearly exams, and use the prayers in this wonderful book."

Amanda Oden Corliss, DVM
Massachusetts

"It is helpful for us to be able to turn to some form of already constructed prayer to help us communicate with God quickly, directly and effectively. *Animal Prayer Guide* is destined to become a basic in any animal-lovers library."

Reverends John & Lauren McLaughlin
Port Richey, Florida

"This is a wonderful, wonderful book! There are so many wondrous and amazing stories and thoughts. I think it's a book like no other. It's one of a kind, and you have been the first person that I know of to be used by God to write it. The fact that it's Scripturally based is of such importance as God's Word is of much more importance than anyone's opinion. You have been such a blessing to me, and to everyone else who will read this book. God Bless You, Niki, for such a wonderful work well done!"

Janis Nedelec
British Columbia, Canada

"Animal Prayer Guide is a moving and insightful book for those who want to pray for their pets and all animals. The scriptures on prayer, faith, and receiving answers from God are a balm for the soul from the Word of God. A blessing and a must read for all animal lovers, just as *There Is Eternal Life For Animals* is."

Ann Chase, President & Founder
Noah's Ark Foundation
Animal Breeder & Trainer
Honor Golden Retrievers, North Carolina

9

Table of Contents

Quick Reference Prayer Directory

Chapter 1

Introduction To Prayer

"Sorrow looks back, worry looks around,
and faith looks up."

Ralph Waldo Emerson

As you read this book you may want to have your Bible handy, because we're going to review the subject of prayer in the Bible. If you believe in God, Jesus Christ, the Holy Spirit, and that the Bible is the Word of God, then you must believe that what it says in the Bible is true. The Bible tells us to pray and shows us that our prayers make a big difference in the outcome of any situation.

Prayer – How Does It Work?

If God chose to do so, He could arbitrarily do things at any given time without assistance from anyone. He does not need people, angels or animals to carry out His will. He is the One Who created all of us, and this world, out of nothing to begin with. However, God has chosen prayer as the mode of operation for communication with Him, and as the driving force of spiritual activity and assistance. All through the Bible we see examples of heavenly intervention through spiritual petitions by people.

God uses His created beings to carry out these actions. These beings are angels, people and animals. But what activates the action by these beings is your prayer and faith. Prayer and faith go hand in hand.

Prayer and faith are the spiritual ingredients of every miracle. What is faith? Hebrews 11:1 says faith is the substance of things hoped for, the evidence of things not seen. Faith is a spirit ("spirit of faith" II Corinthians 4:13) just as fear is a spirit. However, God has not given us the spirit of fear but of a sound mind (II Timothy 1:7).

Romans 12:3&6 says that God has given everyone a measure of faith. We are told that it is impossible to please God without faith (Hebrews 11:6). Paul the apostle said he lives by faith, and they, which be of faith, are blessed along with faithful Abraham (Galatians 2:20 and 3:9). The Bible says that the just shall live by faith (Romans 1:17).

Faith is a spiritual weapon of warfare against the devil. Ephesians 6:16 tells us **"above all, taking the shield of faith, wherewith you will be able to quench all the fiery darts of the wicked."** And verse 18 further teaches us that we should be, **"praying always."**

We already learned that everyone has been given a portion of faith, so how do we increase it? Romans 10:17 says we increase our faith by hearing the Word of God. This means keep hearing it, keep reading it, and stay focused on the spiritual things of God. The Bible says we walk by faith, not by sight (II Corinthians 5:7). Jesus said, "have faith in God." That actually sounds more like a command (Mark 11:22). Jesus said if you can believe, all things are possible (Mark 9:23). Once Paul was speaking about someone who was crippled and he said that he perceived that this person had faith to be healed (Acts 14:9). Therefore, you can see how vital our faith is to the outcome of our requests.

Jesus said to a woman who came to Him asking for healing for her daughter, "great is thy faith: be it unto thee even as thou wilt." And her daughter was made whole from that very hour (Matthew 15:28). This healing was attributed to the woman's faith. Notice that He didn't say, if it's God will for your daughter to be healed, then she'll receive her healing. If we read the Word of God carefully, we'll see that it is always God's will for His creatures to be healed. In fact, Jesus told a story to encourage us to keep asking and don't give up.

There was a widow who continually went to a judge and said avenge me of my adversary. This judge did not fear God, and he didn't care about people. The widow kept asking, coming to his house at any time of day or night. Finally, the judge gave her what she wanted just to get rid of her. Jesus said, if this judge who did not fear God, and did not care about people knew how to give her what she wants, how much more will your Heavenly Father give to His children (Luke 18:1-8). Therefore, Jesus is saying that He doesn't want us to give up just because we haven't gotten the answer yet. Ask and keep asking. This truth in the Word of God refutes the speculation viewed by some people that we don't have any clue or rhyme or reason as to why some get healed and others do not. The teaching of the Bible blows a hole in the all too common perception that healing is not for everyone or every creature.

There are numerous scriptures that show us that faith is the activity that drives the results. Since there are too many to go over in this book, I will reference some examples of verses that state faith brought or will bring the answer, healing or miracle. I encourage you to take a few minutes to read these scriptures.

Matthew 9:20-22, Matthew 15:28, Matthew 21:22, Mark 5:34, Mark 10:52, Mark 11:24, Luke 7:2-10, Luke 8:43-48, and James 5:14-15.

So you can see that God has already made provisions for our answers to prayer by giving us the authority to ask and the expectancy to receive. Each one of us was given a portion of faith to build on. Therefore, it rests on us to activate it. In other words, the ball is now in our court. Somebody once said, show me and I'll believe, but Jesus said believe Me and I'll show you (Mark 9:23).

Does God want us to pray? Yes. In everything, by prayer and petition, with thanksgiving, present your requests to God (Philippians 4:6). And James 5:14-15 tells us that if there are any sick among you they should call the elders of the church to pray. We are told to "pray one for another" in James 5:16.

"He shall call upon Me, and I will answer him: I will be with him in trouble; I will deliver him, and honor him" (Psalm 91:15).

Here are some examples to show you how God uses His creatures in response to prayers. First we'll cover some Bible examples and then some contemporary ones.

Bible Examples

The Use of Angels

Hebrews 12:22 tells us that there are an innumerable company of angels in the heavenlies. In fact, Paul tells us in Hebrews 13:1 that we should be on our toes, because we could be entertaining angels and not be aware of it! We all have angels as Jesus told us in Matthew 18:10.

Three Men Rescued From The Fiery Furnace

King Nebuchadnezzar made a decree that everyone must worship a golden image. Anyone who wouldn't do it would be cast into the midst of a burning fiery furnace. There were three Jews that were set over the affairs of the province of Babylon: Shadrach, Meshach and Abednego. These three men would not obey the king, but preferred to obey God and worship Him only. As a result, they were thrown into the fiery furnace to die. Even the men that threw them into the furnace died, because the heat was turned up seven times more than usual. However, there was an interesting turn of events. King Nebuchadnezzar looked into the furnace, and saw four men in there alive and well. Four men were in there, but only three men were put in! The Bible says that the fourth man was like the Son of God. After this miracle they were set free.

(From Daniel Chapter 3).

16

Peter Rescued From Prison By An Angel

King Herod was pursuing the Christians, and ordered that the Apostle Peter be put in prison. Peter was apprehended and put in prison, but prayer was made by the church without ceasing. While Peter was sleeping in the prison between two soldiers, bound with two chains, and with guards in front of the door, an angel of the Lord came, shined a light on him, hit Peter on his side and raised him up, saying, arise quickly. Then his chains fell off from his hands and the angel said, come and follow me. Peter said, surely I know that the Lord has sent His angel and delivered me out of the hand of Herod.

(From Acts 12:1-10)

The Use of People

God Used the Prophet Isaiah

King Hezekiah became deathly sick with a boil, and the Prophet Isaiah told him to get his house in order because God said he was going to die. But the king turned his face to the wall and prayed, saying, "O Lord, remember now how I have walked before Thee in truth and with a perfect heart, and have done that which is good in Thy sight." And King Hezekiah wept and the Lord took pity on him and sent Isaiah back to tell him this, "I have heard thy prayer, I have seen thy tears: behold, I will heal thee." Then Isaiah said, "take a lump of figs" and they laid it on the boil and he recovered in three days. God also added 15 years to Hezekiah's life.

(From II Kings Chapter 20, Isaiah Chapter 38).

There are a few things to notice about the story of King Hezekiah. One is that he cried out to God and prayed, and God reversed His decision to take Hezekiah home. Many people say, well, when God is ready to take you home, it's your time to die, but you can see how prayer changed this situation even though God intended to take Hezekiah home. God used the Prophet Isaiah to answer his prayers. He didn't get healed instantly, but it took three days, and in this case he used a fig salve to put on the boil. Sometimes God will use a medicinal remedy for healing and other times He won't. Sometimes you get healed instantly, other times you have to wait for a while.

The Use of Animals

Jonah And The Whale

God allowed a whale to swallow Jonah because he was disobedient. Jonah remained in the belly of the whale for three days. Jonah 2:1 says, "Then Jonah prayed unto the Lord his God out of the fish's belly." Then the Lord told the whale to let Jonah go, and the whale vomited him up unharmed as commanded by God (Jonah Chapters 1 & 2). God used the whale to release Jonah in answer to Jonah's prayer.

ELIJAH FED BY THE RAVENS.

God Used a Raven to Help the Prophet Elijah

Elijah had to go into hiding, because there were people that wanted to kill him. While Elijah was in a prayer conversation with God, the Lord gave him these directions.

> Then the Word of the Lord came to Elijah: "Leave here, turn eastward and hide in the Kerith Ravine, east of the Jordan. You will drink from the brook, and I have ordered the ravens to feed you there." So he did what the Lord had told him. He went to the Kerith Ravine, east of the Jordan, and stayed there. The ravens brought him bread and meat in the morning and bread and meat in the evening, and he drank from the brook.
>
> I Kings 17:2-6

Contemporary Examples

The Use of Animals

Saved by the White Cat

> It was a dark, cold wintry night, and the changing weather had caused a fog so dense that you couldn't see more than a foot in front of your car. My friend and I were on our way to visit someone who had given us directions to her house. After half an hour of driving, we realized that we had forgotten to take the paper with the directions on it.
>
> Our friend's new home was located in a remote rural area in the mountains of western Pennsylvania. As we passed the last landmark before her home, we began to count the dirt trails that intersected with the road we were on. We prayed for guidance. When we reached what we believed to be the right one, we turned onto it, and bounced along the road through the forest toward where we thought the house was located.

A few minutes into our drive, a white cat suddenly appeared in front of our car in the center of the trail. It looked through the windshield directly at us through the heavy fog. My friend slammed on the brakes to avoid hitting the cat. Our hearts were in our throats. We were certain that we had hit the cat and that we'd find it under the wheels of the car.

We got out of the car to look for the cat, but it wasn't there. We hadn't seen it move from the spot where it stood in the center of the road, and we were practically on top of it before we realized it was there. I walked behind the car to look, but the cat wasn't there. I then decided to walk up ahead of the car for a bit to see if I could locate it.

That's when I made the discovery that the cat had saved our lives. Not more than five feet in front of where the car had stopped was the edge of a cliff. There was no barrier – just a steep drop off the side of the mountain. We searched and searched, but never found the cat. That dear, sweet, beautiful animal had been a guardian angel to the two of us that night.

(Author: Marjorie)

Child Prays for a Cat of Her Own

Dwight Nelson told a true story about a pastor. He had a kitten that climbed up a tree in his backyard and then was afraid to come down. The pastor coaxed, offered warm milk, and tried his best to get the kitten down. The kitty just would not come down.

The tree was not sturdy enough to climb, so the pastor decided that if he tied a rope to his car and the tree and drove away so that the tree bent down, he could then reach up and get the kitten. He did all this, checking his progress in the car frequently, then figured if he went just a little bit further, the tree would be bent sufficiently for him to reach the kitten. But as he moved a little further forward, the rope broke. The tree went "boing!" and the kitten instantly sailed through the air and went out of sight.

The pastor felt terrible. He walked all over the neighborhood asking people if they'd seen a little kitten. No, no one had seen a stray kitten. So he prayed, "Lord, I just commit this kitten to Your keeping," and went on about his business.

A few days later he was at the grocery store, and met one of his church members. He happened to look into her shopping cart, and was amazed to see cat food. Now this woman was a cat hater and everyone knew it, so he asked her, "Why are you buying cat food when you hate cats so much?"

She replied, "You won't believe this," and told him how her little girl had been begging her for a cat, but she kept refusing. Then a few days before, the child had begged again, so the mom finally told her little girl, "Well, if God gives you a cat, I'll let you keep it." (You can see where this is going ….) She told the pastor, "I watched my child go out in the yard, get on her knees, and ask God for a cat. And really, Pastor, you won't believe this, but I saw it with my own eyes. A kitten suddenly came flying out of the blue sky, with its paws spread out, and landed right in front of her."

The Use of People

Author's Mother, Christine Behrikis

Woman Healed of Cancer (Niki's Mother)

My mother was diagnosed with Non-Hodgkin's Lymphoma (NHL), which is treatable, but fast moving. As soon as we heard about it, we prayed with her on the telephone and then, my husband Jack and I went to see her. We anointed her with oil and prayed together. Jesus said, "Where two or three are gathered in My Name, there am I in the midst of them." Praise God that Jesus was there and answered our prayers! She began chemo treatments, and the family fasted and prayed standing on the Word of God. Many people joined in to pray for her from all over the country, including her church and other ministries.

After three chemo treatments my mother had another scan. The next day the doctor telephoned her to tell her that her scan looked very good. He said it looked all cleared up, and what they believe they can still see looks like scar tissue. He said he wanted her to have another three chemo treatments, and finish the protocol. Then they would do another scan.

After her treatments were completed, she had another scan and it confirmed that the cancer was gone! Praise God for answered prayer! This is a great, big victory and we give the glory to God! Someone said it was the chemo plus prayer that healed her, but I say it was prayer plus the chemo!

Pete Shanahan

Long Feline Life – Niki and Jack's cat, Pete

Jack and I continually prayed for our cat, Pete, during his life. Even with urinary tract problems in which he was blocked and very ill, which is life threatening if left untreated quickly, an enlarged heart, veterinarians told us his kidneys were small, and in his senior years he developed kidney disease, God blessed Pete and he lived to be over 21 years old. This is considered a long life for a cat.

When we learned that Pete's kidneys were in trouble, we fasted often once a week, anointed Pete with oil, and prayed for him daily. We kept track of his creatine and BUN readings, gave him one Tumil-K potassium pill a day and kept praying.

This went on for a few years until he finally became lethargic, and had to be rushed to the hospital when he was 21 years old.   Then we gave him fluids with vitamin B in it every day, and God gave us another ten

23

months with him. Pete had an excellent quality of life, and was always happy throughout his years here on earth with us. God used Jack and me and our prayers and faith to bless Pete, and Pete was a great blessing to us! Today, Pete is still very much alive and well in heaven! God preserves man and animals (Psalm 36:6).

Food Provided For Large Family In Need

When evangelist R. W. Schambach was a child his family was having hard times. His mother was having difficulty keeping food on the table for the family of twelve children. One day they sat at the table with empty plates and a cold stove while she prayed and thanked God for the food. The kids thought Mom was going crazy because there was no food, the stove was cold, the table was set, and she was saying grace to thank God for their food.

Suddenly the door opened and it was a lady from her church who said, the Lord told me to make this dinner for you and bring it over. In she came with a complete meal for the whole family. Then they realized that Mom wasn't crazy after all. She just had faith in God, because faith is the substance of things hoped for, the evidence of things not seen (Hebrews 11:1).

Cat Healed

Our prayer group received a request to pray for a cat named Nora who went into the hospital with possible liver failure, and she had already been diagnosed with kidney failure. We prayed for Nora and miraculously her lab tests looked like they belonged to a different cat, and she became a feisty ball of energy. Pretty remarkable! She went home the next day. It looked more like pancreatitis, but her liver enzymes were fine, her kidney enzymes were fine, there was no protein in her urine, but she had a bit of an infection.

Her mom, Kari, said; "only a miracle can really explain it, because there are enough similarities (plus how she looked) to make us think it wasn't a lab error." No one at the vet's office could believe it! She went from near comatose to great overnight, and has stayed that way! Her lab tests have continued to be great! – Virtually everything within normal limits. She was on antibiotics and some periactin for her appetite, and, of course, fluids twice a week. Her kidney enzymes, however, are absolutely perfect. They think it was low-grade pancreatitis and a miracle!

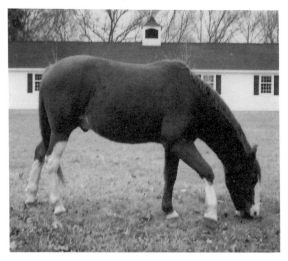

John Wesley and His Horse Are Healed Simultaneously

John Wesley (1703-91) was an evangelist and founder of Methodism. He studied at Oxford, and was ordained a deacon and then a priest, and in 1726 became a fellow at Oxford and lecturer in Greek. His Bible commentaries and sermons are of the most highly respected theologians of all time. I want to show you something that you may never have heard about John Wesley. In reading his journal, I have found that he really loved animals. He lived in a day when travel was only done on horseback. His ministry called him to travel constantly, and he had many stories and adventures along the way. Here is one of them.

"It was Monday, March 17, 1746. I took my leave of Newcastle and set out with Mr. Downes and Mr. Shepherd. But when we came to the town of Smeton, Mr. Downes was so ill that he could go no further. When Mr. Shepherd and I left Smeton, my horse was so exceedingly lame that I was afraid I would have to stay behind, too. We could not figure out what it was that was wrong; and yet he would scarcely set his foot to the ground. By the time I had ridden seven miles, I was thoroughly tired and my head ached more than it had done for some months.

What happened here is fact, for let every man account for it as he sees good. I then thought, cannot God heal either man or beast, by any means, or without any? Immediately my weariness and headache ceased, and so did my horse's lameness in the same instant. Nor did he halt any more either that day or the next."

(From John Wesley's personal journal – paraphrased for ease of understanding.)

The Use of Angels

Angels Protected Niki's Dad

My father told us a story many years ago about how he and another minister were on their way to a church service. They got lost and pulled over to use a public telephone (this was long before cell phones were invented). The neighborhood was rough and there were several people around that looked threatening. They prayed quickly to themselves for God's protection. While my Dad and the other man were at the phone, a couple of big, ominous looking men came up to them as if they would start trouble. My Dad said it was the most amazing thing, because these men looked at my

Dad, they looked at his friend, and then they looked beside them and up a little higher as though they saw other men with them that were much bigger than my Dad, who was 6 feet tall. Immediately, they turned around and left.

My Dad is convinced that there were angels standing there protecting them. My Dad and his friend couldn't see the angels. But God gave these other men the ability to see into the spiritual world. They saw these angels standing there who appeared as men who were stronger than them, and it put fear into their hearts. There are scores of stories about how angelic beings have come to the rescue of people, and most assuredly, there are incidences where angels have helped us and we haven't even had a clue that they did so.

Jesus Himself

Man Healed of Spinal Meningitis, Coma, and Rheumatoid Arthritis

R. W. Schambach met a man who told him the story of how he was dying in the hospital. The man was in a coma, dying of spinal meningitis. Rheumatoid arthritis had set in everywhere in his body. The medical bills were so high that they had to sell the house to pay them.

Then one day a priest came in to his hospital room through the door wearing all black, and gave him his last rights. He could understand everything going on, but he had no ability to respond to the priest.

Right after the priest left, another priest came in the room. But this one wore all white and he walked through the wall! He bent down and whispered in the dying man's ear and said, **"You don't have any trouble, all you need is faith in God."** He said, "I am Jesus of Nazareth and I'm going to heal you. I want you to get up and wash yourself and shave. Leave this hospital and buy a Bible and start reading in the Gospel of John and you will find the way to eternal life" – and he did so, and he was healed, and found the way to eternal life!

I hope these stories have inspired you to believe God for the miracle you need. Let's believe God and His Word over our circumstances, over what we see, what we feel and what we hear. You see there are two opposing forces: faith and fear. One works against the other – one cancels out the other. When we pay attention to negative things, which may be found on the TV, radio, and newspapers or from people, the negative communication works like an eraser on a whiteboard and wipes off all the faith that you have built up. Evangelist Jesse Duplantis says, "Fear tolerated is faith contaminated." Fear is really faith in reverse. Someone once said, "If you're going to worry, why pray, and if you're going to pray, why worry?"

Chapter 2

Prayer Overview

We can ask God to take care of our animal companions and all the animals of the world just as freely as we can ask for ourselves. We are their caretakers and can and should pray on their behalf. Adam was the caretaker of all the animals in the Garden of Eden, and God told him to give them names. Did you know that your animal companion is part of your household? Yes, of course, you look at it that way, but did you know that God does, too? Look at this Bible verse, which tells us that our pets are part of our household.

Six days you shall labor and do all your work, but the seventh day is a Sabbath to the Lord your God. On it you shall not do any work, neither you, nor your son or daughter, nor your manservant or maidservant, nor your animals, nor the alien within your gates.

Exodus 20:9-10 NIV

I would like to say a word about the Old Testament scriptures. Keep in mind that when you read passages from the Old Testament that were directed to God's people, the Israelites, that if you are a Christian, you have become one of God's people, too. Remember that when Jesus came here to save the world, that He "opened enrollment" to all people of all nations who want to live for Him. Therefore, you can claim all the promises in the Word of God for yourself, and your loved ones, whether it is found in the Old or New Testaments.

In the following verse there is no question that God is telling us that if we serve God and obey Him, not only will we be blessed, but all our children and all our beloved animals will be blessed also. Therefore, don't ever let anyone tell you that God won't bless or heal your pet or that He doesn't want to. **Here is solid proof that He wants to!**

If you fully obey the Lord your God and carefully follow all His commands I give you today, the Lord your God will set you high above all the nations on earth. **All these blessings will come upon you and accompany you if you obey the Lord your God:**

You will be blessed in the city and blessed in the country. The fruit of your womb will be blessed, and the crops of your land and **the young of your livestock – the calves of your herds and the lambs of your flocks.**

Deuteronomy 28:1-4 NIV

There are many promises in the Word of God, which state that God will give us the desires of our heart, and invite us to ask for what we desire. God said He is **"a rewarder of them that diligently seek Him,"** and that we should **"ask and ye shall**

receive that your joy may be full." The following scriptures are solid evidence that:

- God invites us to ask Him for what we want.
- God wants us to have what we desire, and He wants us to be happy and joyful.
- God keeps His promises.
- God will continue to keep His promises in heaven.
- God will keep His promises forever.

The following are only some of the scriptures that promise to give us what we ask for:

Hitherto have ye asked nothing in My name: ask, and ye shall receive, that your joy may be full.

John 16:24

If ye abide in Me, and My words abide in you, ye shall ask what ye will, and it shall be done unto you.

John 15:7

He that spared not His own Son, but delivered Him up for us all, how shall He not with Him also freely give us all things?

Romans 8:32

Be careful for nothing; but in every thing by prayer and supplication with thanksgiving let your requests be made known unto God.

Philippians 4:6

The next verse tells us that we should have confidence in God that if we ask Him for anything, He will do it. It also makes the statement that if we ask "according to His will," He will hear us and do it. We already know it is His will to help us, to do what we desire, and there are certainly many scriptures that state that He wants to heal us.

In fact, everywhere Jesus went, He healed the sick. If you have any questions about whether or not God wants to heal you or your household, I recommend the book *Healing The Sick* by T. L. Osborn. The Word of God tells us that God always wants to heal you. Obviously, we should never ask or expect to receive something which is sinful or against God's teachings.

> And this is the confidence that we have in Him, that, if we ask any thing according to His will, He heareth us: And if we know that He hear us, whatsoever we ask, we know that we have the petitions that we desired of Him.
>
> I John 5:14-15

> He Himself bore our sins in His body on the tree, so that we might die to sins and live for righteousness; by His wounds you have been healed.
>
> I Peter 2:24 NIV

> Praise the Lord, O my soul, and forget not all His benefits – who forgives all your sins and heals all your diseases ...
>
> Psalm 103:2-3 NIV

Will God make all His promises good?

> God is not a man, that He should lie, nor a son of man, that He should change His mind. Does He speak and then not act? Does He promise and not fulfill?
>
> Numbers 23:19 NIV

> For no matter how many promises God has made, they are "Yes" in Christ. And so through Him the "Amen" is spoken by us to the glory of God.
>
> II Corinthians 1:20 NIV

But without faith it is impossible to please Him: for he that cometh to God must believe that He is, and that He is a rewarder of them that diligently seek Him.

Hebrews 11:6

Are the promises still good when we get to heaven?

And I will give unto thee the keys of the kingdom of heaven: and whatsoever thou shalt bind on earth shall be bound in heaven: and whatsoever thou shalt loose on earth shall be loosed in heaven.

Matthew 16:19

Verily I say unto you, Whatsoever ye shall bind on earth shall be bound in heaven: and whatsoever ye shall loose on earth shall be loosed in heaven.

Matthew 18:18

How long are the promises good?

But the Word of the Lord endureth for ever. And this is the Word which by the gospel is preached unto you.

I Peter 1:25

The grass withers, and the flowers fall, but the Word of our God stands forever.

Isaiah 40:8 NIV

For ever, O Lord, Thy Word is settled in heaven.

Psalm 119:89

Heaven and earth shall pass away, but My Words shall not pass away.

Matthew 24:35

We are instructed by God to ask for what we need. In Philippians 4:6 it tells us that by prayer and petition we should present our requests to God with thanksgiving.

There are many wonderful scriptures to use when praying for animals, however, these are just a few of them. Any scripture that you can claim for yourself can be used to benefit your pet. In other words, if the scripture says He will give you the desires of your heart or do anything you ask, then you can ask for healing for your pet.

I recommend praying for everything, saying grace over their food, pray about which veterinarian to go to (it does make a difference), pray before you leave to go to the veterinarian, especially if there is a real problem, and pray about what kind of food to give them. Remember to say "Thank You" too, for God's blessings.

I have some model prayers in this book, which you are welcome to use and customize to your own needs. Prayer should always be from the heart, therefore, these have been written just to give you some guidance.

As different needs arise for you and your family, you should always ask the Lord for help. No request is too great or too small or insignificant for God. One aspect that I hope to introduce to you is to use the Bible promises right in your prayer request. In other words, stand on the promises of God and be relentless.

There are some things that you can do to strengthen your prayer efforts. I have outlined some suggestions here.

First, one should always ask God for forgiveness for any sins. You always want to start out with a "clean slate" so to speak. This is a daily task since we are human and make mistakes constantly.

If you haven't committed your life to the Lord, and would like to do so, please go to the prayer at the end of this book. We have studied in the book *There Is Eternal Life For Animals* that all of the animals go to heaven according to the Bible, and we want to make sure that we are there to be with them!

Write a list of the things you want to pray about and add to it as you think of new requests. Prayer for your pets, family, job, anything that concerns you, will concern the Lord. Asking the Lord for help on everything is a good habit to develop. For example, to help you find the right job, spouse, car, computer, doctors and veterinarians.

We all need money to live on, so there's nothing wrong with asking God to help you financially. As long as you are not asking for something that is wrong or sinful, there is no reason why you can't do so. My Dad once had a discussion with a lady who said "I don't believe in asking God for money, and I would never do it." My Dad, never at a loss for a quick comeback, said, "I'm not only going to ask God to help me financially, but I'm going to ask God for the money that He would have given you if you asked Him, too!"

Your biggest asset is prayer! In fact, the Bible says to pray without ceasing (I Thessalonians 5:17).

Fasting and prayer are often mentioned in the Bible as ways to strengthen your requests. You could fast one day, drinking only beverages. Then take out your list of prayer requests and pray alone or with a prayer partner. Don't forget to thank God for all He has done and is about to do for you.

Holy Communion

You can also have your own communion using grape juice and a cracker. However, an absolute must – you need to ask God's forgiveness when you have communion (I Corinthians 11:23-34).

Holy Communion Prayer

Dear Lord,

Please forgive me of all sins, and make me a blessing for the glory of God. Thank you for Your sacrifice of dying for our sins and for Your resurrection that brings us eternal life. Amen!

Bible verse to read while having Holy Communion.

While they were eating, Jesus took bread, gave thanks and broke it, and gave it to His disciples, saying, "Take and eat; this is My body." Then He took the cup, gave thanks and offered it to them, saying, "Drink from it, all of you. This is my blood of the covenant, which is poured out for many for the forgiveness of sins."

Matthew 26:26-28 NIV

Then you can read some other Bible scriptures for your devotional time. If you don't know where to read, you could start with the Gospel of John found in the New Testament, which is the fourth book. Also, the whole book of Psalms is wonderful to read.

The way that we like to do this is to start with communion, then we go through our prayer list, and then we end by reading some scriptures.

Anointing with oil symbolizes the Holy Spirit. You can anoint your pet with oil. It's not the oil in itself that heals, but it represents the Holy Spirit. People usually put a little oil on the forehead before praying (Reference scriptures: Mark 6:13 and James 5:14-15).

Here are a few Bible verses to encourage you to ask God for help.

He that spared not His own Son, but delivered Him up for us all, how shall He not with Him also freely give us all things?

Romans 8:32

God is our refuge and strength, a very present help in trouble.

Psalm 46:1

Bless the Lord, O my soul, and forget not all His benefits: who forgiveth all thine iniquities; who healeth all thy diseases.

Psalm 103:2-3

... I am the Lord that healeth thee.

Exodus 15:26

Delight yourself in the Lord and He will give you the desires of your heart.

Psalm 37:4 NIV

Ask and it will be given to you; seek and you will find; knock and the door will be opened to you. For everyone who asks receives; he who seeks finds; and to him who knocks, the door will be opened.

Matthew 7:7-8 NIV

Let us therefore come boldly unto the throne of grace, that we may obtain mercy, and find grace to help in time of need.

Hebrews 4:16

Therefore I tell you, whatever you ask for in prayer, believe that you have received it, and it will be yours.

Mark 11:24 NIV

Chapter 3

Special Prayers For Our Animal Companions

Not all the archangels can tell
The joys of that holiest place,
Where the Father is pleased to reveal
The light of His heavenly face.

Charles Wesley

The best advice we can possibly receive is from Jesus Christ Himself. The disciples said to Jesus, teach us to pray, and this is the "Our Father" prayer that Jesus gave them.

The Our Father

After this manner therefore pray ye: Our Father which art in heaven, Hallowed be Thy Name. Thy kingdom come. Thy will be done in earth, as it is in heaven. Give us this day our daily bread. And forgive us our debts, as we forgive our debtors. And lead us not into temptation, but deliver us from evil: For Thine is the kingdom, and the power, and the glory, for ever. Amen.

Matthew 6:9-13

Saying Grace Over Your Pet's Food

Thou openest Thine Hand,
And satisfieth the desire of every living thing.

Psalm 145:16

It's important to say grace over your pet's food and water at each feeding every day. You want God to bless any food and water that your animal companion is about to consume. The first two interesting stories came from a book called *Man and Beast: Here and Hereafter* by Rev. J. G. Wood, which was published in 1874.

Rev. John George Wood (1827-1889) was born in London. Because he was rather sickly as a child, he was educated at home and spent a great deal of time outdoors. During this time he developed his innate love of all of God's creation. In 1854 he was ordained a priest. He delivered occasional lectures on natural history subjects, and wrote numerous books on animals, plants and nature.

Your animal companion's food and water are very important. Perhaps I can show you what I mean by sharing these cute stories.

A Cat Feeds A Dog

In the hot weather our large dog, Nelly, used to be chained under a large oak tree in the grounds at the back of the house, just within sight of her kennel and the yard door. This was done that she might have the comfort of the cool position during the heat of the day, and at the same time command the back entrance to the house. This, however, took her away from the neighborhood of the cook, and the little scraps and dainty bits, which used to be given to her now and then while the different meals were in course of preparation.

At the same time, we had a dear motherly old cat, who did not approve of the change of position in which her friend, Nelly, was placed. Still less did she approve of the cook putting all the scraps in a plate, instead of giving them to Nelly. So she set herself to work at conveying them to her friend, and everything that was not too large for the cat to carry or drag along, she took to the dog under the tree, and seemed delighted when she saw her friend eat them.

Now she never stole anything for herself, but she would always do so for any of the dogs. She used to carry little treats to a small dog that was chained up in the house, but this was after she developed the plan of helping Nelly to the dainties of which she, in her pussy-cat brain, considered her friend to have been defrauded.

I'm sure this little cat has a special place of recognition in heaven; because she practiced God's scripture that says it is more blessed to give than to receive. Here's another story from J. G. Wood's book about a horse and how important his water was to him!

A Horse That Pumps His Own Water

The pump to the water was in the corner of the horse-box in which the horse was shut for the night. The coachman used to be puzzled at the fact that when he came in the morning the end of the stable was always an inch or so deep in water. At last he suspected that the horse might have been delinquent, and so fastened him up without giving him any water, and watched him unobserved when let loose in the morning. The animal went at once to the pump, took the handle in his teeth, worked it up and down, and, when the water was in full flow, placed his mouth under the spout to drink. He could not endure being watched while pumping, and, if he saw anyone observing him, would rush at him with open mouth in order to scare them away.

A Raccoon Gets His Own Snacks

A woman in Pennsylvania has a pet raccoon named Bandit. He likes to eat snacks like chips and cheese. When his owner decided he needed to go on a diet, she locked up Bandit's favorite peanut butter snacks behind a sliding bolt. Undeterred, he figured out how to lift the handle and slide the bolt. Raised around dogs, Bandit even tried to bark like them, said his owner.

Those are great stories about the importance of every creature's food and water. Here are some Bible readings, and then we'll say grace over our pet's food.

Bible Readings

Jesus Feeds The 5,000

Here is a boy with five small barley loaves and two small fish, but how far will they go among so many? Jesus said, "Have the people sit down." There was plenty of grass in that place, and the men sat down, about five thousand of them. Jesus then took the loaves, gave thanks, and distributed to those who were seated as much as they wanted. He did the same with the fish.

John 6:9-11 NIV

Who provides food for the raven when its young cry out to God and wander about for lack of food?

Job 38:41 NIV

He provides food for those who fear Him; He remembers His covenant forever.

Psalm 111:5 NIV

He provides food for the cattle and for the young ravens when they call.

Psalm 147:9 NIV

The lions roar for their prey and seek their food from God.

Psalm 104:21 NIV

I will provide grass in the fields for your cattle, and you will eat and be satisfied.

Deuteronomy 11:15 NIV

This next verse was spoken by God to Noah in preparation for their time in the ark with his family and all the animals.

You are to take every kind of food that is to be eaten and store it away as food for you and for them.

Genesis 6:21 NIV

Give us this day our daily bread.

Matthew 6:11

And my God will meet all your needs according to His glorious riches in Christ Jesus.

Philippians 4:19 NIV

Grace Over Your Pet's Food

Dear Heavenly Father,

We come before You in the Name of Jesus and ask You to please bless this food and water that nourishes [name] to maintain their perfect health. Heal them of all ailments, and bring great blessings, happiness, and soundness of mind. We thank You that You give food to the hungry as Your Word says in Psalm 146:7. Bless them with a very long, healthy, abundant, and happy life with us. We thank You in the Name of The Father, The Son and The Holy Spirit. Amen.

Janis Nedelec's rabbit, Cuddles

I sing the goodness of the Lord,
That filled the earth with food;
He formed the creatures with His Word,
And then pronounced them good.
Lord, how Thy wonders are displayed,
Wherever I turn my eye:
If I survey the ground I tread,
Or gaze upon the sky!

Isaac Watts, 1674-1748
– From the Hymn "I Sing The Mighty Power Of God"

Daily Prayer For Your Pet

Blessed be the Lord, who daily loadeth us with benefits,
even the God of our salvation.

Psalm 68:19

Every aspect of your animal companion's life is important to you, to God, and to himself or herself. We may not always have time to say a lengthy prayer everyday, but remember to pray for your beloved animal companion daily.

Our cat, Lukie

Every day is a new joy and adventure with our pets. There are certain things that my cat, Lukie, likes to help me with each day. One of them is making the bed. He can be downstairs in the house, and with his sharp ears he hears me making the bed. He likes to help me make the bed by jumping up on it while I'm in the middle of making it. So then we stop to kiss and talk and I think, OK, I'll finish making it later. Lukie likes to help me make salad. He walks around me and rubs my legs, gets his kisses, and gets to eat a small piece of lettuce or spinach. He eats it out of my hand, and looks like a little deer munching on his greens.

Bible Readings

In the morning, O Lord, You hear my voice; in the morning I lay my requests before You and wait in expectation.

Psalm 5:3 NIV

Show me Your ways, O Lord, teach me Your paths; guide me in Your truth and teach me, for You are God my Savior, and my hope is in You all day long.

Psalm 25:4-5 NIV

By day the Lord directs His love, at night His song is with me – a prayer to the God of my life.

Psalm 42:8 NIV

But I call to God, and the Lord saves me. Evening, morning and noon I cry out in distress, and He hears my voice.

Psalm 55:16-17 NIV

Sing to the Lord a new song; sing to the Lord, all the earth. Sing to the Lord, praise His name; proclaim His salvation day after day.

Psalm 96:1-2 NIV

Let the morning bring me word of Your unfailing love, for I have put my trust in You. Show me the way I should go, for to You I lift up my soul.

Psalm 143:8 NIV

Every day I will praise You and extol Your name for ever and ever.

Psalm 145:2 NIV

Daily Prayer For Your Pet

Dear Heavenly Father,

We come before You with praise, honor and glory. May all of Your beautiful animal creatures praise Your Name! May You shine Your face upon our beloved animal companions, and show them that Your love is greater than anything that we can imagine.

We pray in the Name of Jesus that we would find great favor with You today that You would please:

Heal [name] from all sickness and disease that they may have even if we are unaware that they have it. Do not allow any sickness, disease, accidents, harm or danger to come upon [name]. Disable all the powers of enemies that would come against them.

Pour out Your blessings upon them that they will have a very long, healthy, happy, and abundant life with us for the Glory of God. Let Your angels watch over them, guide them, and keep them safe continually. Put the hedge of Your protection around them at all times.

Lead and guide us to take the best possible care of [name] and be very responsible pet parents. Direct us to the very best veterinarian that will benefit [name] the most. Show us the correct foods to give them. Help us to keep our cats indoors so they won't get hit by cars, be exposed to diseases and attacks by raccoons, coyotes and other animals or get lost. Protect them when they travel by car, foot, air or any other means.

Give [name] a peaceful spirit of gentleness like the lion that sits beside the lamb, a peace that only comes from God.

We thank you that [name] will go to heaven with us when it is time to cross over to the other side, and we pray that You will bless us also to go to heaven when our time comes. Please let us be joined together again in heaven, and let us live for eternity with [name] in a wonderful home where we will be happy together forever.

We give You the praise, thanksgiving, honor and the glory in the Name of The Father, The Son, and The Holy Spirit. Amen.

Then shall the earth yield her increase;
and God, even our own God, shall bless us.

Psalm 67:6

We love Him, because He first loved us.
I John 4:19

Prayers for the Healing
Of Your Animal Companion

Pray often, for prayer is a shield to the soul,
A sacrifice to God,
And a scourge for Satan.

John Bunyan

Photo of Pete Shanahan, who looks like he's praying!

God does not put sickness on anyone. He wants all of us to be well. If you look at the life of Jesus and His ministry, you will see that He spent the majority of His time healing people of their sicknesses. (References are: Matthew 4:23-24, Luke 4:40, and Matthew 14:14.) He also said that if you have seen Me, you have seen The Father, meaning God The Father and God The Son, Jesus, both agree on everything that He is doing. (See John 14:9.) This tells us very plainly and clearly that God does not put sickness on us, and He does not want any of His creatures to be sick. If you are still unclear about if God wants us all well, or if you want to learn more about healing and the Bible, I recommend the book *Healing The Sick* by T. L. Osborn. It's the best book on the subject that I've ever read.

Jesus taught us to pray and keep praying. He instructs us to persevere and not to give up.

Bible Readings

A Blind Beggar Receives His Sight

> As Jesus approached Jericho, a blind man was sitting by the roadside begging. When he heard the crowd going by, he asked what was happening. They told him, "Jesus of Nazareth is passing by." He called out, "Jesus, Son of David, have mercy on me!" Those who led the way rebuked him and told him to be quiet, but he shouted all the more, "Son of David, have mercy on me!" Jesus stopped and ordered the man to be brought to Him. When he came near, Jesus asked him, "What do you want Me to do for you?" "Lord, I want to see," he replied. Jesus said to him, "Receive your sight; your faith has healed you." Immediately he received his sight and followed Jesus, praising God. When all the people saw it, they also praised God.
>
> Luke 18:35-43 NIV

> ... I tell you the truth, if you have faith as small as a mustard seed, you can say to this mountain, 'Move from here to there' and it will move. Nothing will be impossible for you.
>
> Matthew 17:20 NIV

Now in this next verse Jesus is telling us that **all believers** can pray for healing and miracles.

> Verily, verily, I say unto you, he that believeth on Me, the works that I do shall he do also; and greater works than these shall he do; because I go unto My Father. And whatsoever ye shall ask in My name, that will I do, that the Father may be glorified in the Son. If ye shall ask any thing in My name, I will do it.
>
> John 14:12-14

> And this is the confidence that we have in Him, that, if we ask any thing according to His will, He heareth us:

And if we know that He hear us, whatsoever we ask, we know that we have the petitions that we desired of Him.

I John 5:14-15

Verily I say unto you, whatsoever ye shall bind on earth shall be bound in heaven: and whatsoever ye shall loose on earth shall be loosed in heaven. Again I say unto you, that if two of you shall agree on earth as touching any thing that they shall ask, it shall be done for them of My Father which is in heaven. For where two or three are gathered together in My name, there am I in the midst of them.

Matthew 18:18-20

God is our refuge and strength, a **very present help in trouble.**

Psalm 46:1 (Right now help!)

Bless the Lord, O my soul, and forget not all His benefits: Who forgiveth all thine iniquities; Who healeth all thy diseases.

Psalm 103:2-3

But He was wounded for our transgressions, He was bruised for our iniquities: the chastisement of our peace was upon Him; and with His stripes we are healed.

Isaiah 53:5

But when he asks, he must believe and not doubt, because he who doubts is like a wave of the sea, blown and tossed by the wind. That man should not think he will receive anything from the Lord.

James 1:6-7 NIV

You can anoint your animal companion with oil and then pray.

Prayer For Healing

Dear Heavenly Father,

We come before You with praise, honor and glory. We pray in the Name of Jesus that we would find great favor with You today that You would please: Heal [name] from all sickness and disease. Especially we ask that You would bless and heal [name] [mention particular area of need right now]. Breathe Your healing touch upon [name] today and renew [his/her] body completely.

Do not allow any other sickness or disease to come upon [him/her]. For we know that You are the Lord our God who heals us as You state in Exodus 15:26. Watch over [name] continually and bring great blessings to [her/him]. We know that Jesus was moved with compassion and healed the sick (Matthew 14:14). Guide every doctor, nurse, technician or anyone else who does anything for [name] to ensure that [she/he] is very well taken care of.

Disable all the powers of the devil. Let your angels watch over [name] to guide [him/her] and keep [her/him] safe. Put a hedge of protection around [name] at all times. We ask that You would bless [name] with a very long, healthy, happy, and abundant life with [pet parents].

Bless [pet parents] and help them to go through this as calmly as possible, and let [pet parents] know that You are not only with them, but You are with [name]! We give You the praise, thanksgiving, honor and glory in the Name of The Father, The Son, and The Holy Spirit. Amen.

> But they that wait upon the Lord
> Shall renew their strength;
> They shall mount up with wings as eagles;
> They shall run, and not be weary;
> And they shall walk, and not faint.
>
> Isaiah 40:31

Chapter 4

Prayer For Animals Everywhere

Let them praise the Name of the Lord: for He commanded, and
they were created.

Psalm 148:5

There are ways that we can help all the animals in the world in
our own little way. Praying for them is a very important way
to help them. We can ask God to intercede on their behalf for
safety and protection. You should also look into signing
petitions that contribute to the well being of animals, such as
the Doris Day Animal League causes. You can donate money,
food, litter, toys, blankets, and volunteer time to a local animal
shelter. Monetary donations are always welcome, and I would
encourage you to donate to no-kill shelters. Never leave any
animal at a shelter that does not have a no-kill policy. There
are many sad stories that can be told about animals that were
euthanized because they weren't adopted quick enough, and
you don't want to create another one.

I would also suggest that wildlife should not be left with a pet
shelter. They are not equipped to handle them and may

euthanize them. You may have to do some calling and scouting around to find a way to help them. Try looking up wildlife centers on the internet for guidance.

Another way to help animals is to feed the birds in your yard. We love to feed the birds and our cats, Lukie and Joey, have a great time watching them fly around. We use sunflower seeds because it seems to be a favorite for most birds, including blue jays and cardinals. I think it's best to keep the feeders a reasonable distance from your house. When we first started to feed the birds we kept a bird feeder on our deck. I was so surprised one day when I walked into our living room and saw my cat, Luke, looking out the atrium door right into the eyes of a squirrel! They were both starring at each other on either side of the window, and I wished that I had a camera with me at that moment.

According to a Stanford Alumni Association essay, feeding backyard birds began in earnest in the 1950's. They say that feeding may pull many birds, especially weak individuals, through the extremes of the winter.

Some people like to feed ducks. One day when my friend and I were coming out of a restaurant some of the employees that worked there were feeding some ducks. There was a pond right on the property. I opened my car door, and my friend and I were so engrossed in watching the ducks being fed that we walked toward the back of the car and watched them. Then suddenly as I faced the ducks and my friend faced my car with the door open, she said to me "there's a duck in your car! It's sitting in the driver's seat. Oh, he just got out of the car." We went back into the car looking very carefully to make sure there weren't any ducks in there. I wish I saw the duck sitting in my driver's seat!

Here are some stories about people helping animals in need.

Horses Spared

A wild horse preserve operator named Slick in California recently rescued 500 horses. These horses were in danger of being seized and put into slaughterhouses. Some of these horses were sent to a refuge in Texas, and others were sent to a ranch in California. We are thankful for the loving and caring individuals that help our beautiful animal creatures, and spare them from death and cruelty. Thank the Lord for caring people like these folks.

Twenty Pets Rescued From A Flood

A 'random act of kindness' during a flood saved the lives of 20 pets living at the Versailles Condominium Complex in Hudson, Ohio. Local veterinary technician Diane organized a rescue effort by calling the Hudson Police Department to gain access to the complex, and the owner of the Chalet, a local pet boarding and grooming facility.

Chalet owner Susan agreed to help by housing the displaced animals and lent Diane a pole and some gloves to use in the rescue effort. Diane pestered the police from 8:00 in the morning until 2:00 p.m. that day, when police sergeant Rob Walker escorted her into the building to search for animals trapped inside. In the interim, she went to the local high school, where evacuees from the condominium complex were taken, to obtain a list of pets.

During the next seven hours, Diane rescued pets from remote hiding spots such as piles of debris and the springs under sofas and mattresses. She made three drop-offs to the Chalet that evening by nine o'clock. One particularly brave cat, a white female named Lily, remained fearless throughout the entire rescue operation. She greeted Diane by rubbing against her ankles and purring, and when asked, went into her carrier without a struggle.

Hudson police Sgt. John E. Lowman said Diane was the flood's only creature guardian angel. "We were thankful. You can plan for only so much," he said. "We didn't expect for three apartment buildings to become uninhabitable. A lot of elderly people live there, and that's all they had were their animals. She's an unsung hero."

Desperate Duck Saved

A female mallard duck in Scotland was recently plucked from the jaws of death by two engineers after being sucked in from the sea through a pipe into a power station's water tower. The men, using only a rope, a couple of coat hangers and a healthy dose of Scottish ingenuity, rescued the duck after workers at Cockenzie Power Station in East Lothian heard a distressed squawking inside the tower at 8:00 a.m. The frightened duck was bobbing around 20 feet down inside the shaft, in imminent danger of getting squashed in the crushing machine.

The workers immediately contacted the Scottish Society for the Prevention of Cruelty to Animals

(SSPCA) to help rescue the duck. "When the SSPCA had difficulty, we called the fire brigade around lunchtime but they found the situation impossible as well, because the duck kept diving away from their nets," according to a spokesperson for Scottish Power, which owns the power station.

Seven hours later, the duck was still enduring her terrifying ordeal. But at last, engineers Brian and Jimmy came up with an ingenious solution. "They put a piece of rope with a lasso inside a 25-foot long piece of pipe to stop it from blowing about. They managed to hoop it over the bird's neck and pulled it back up the shaft gently so as not to injure the creature," the Scottish Power spokesman said. "It was getting a bit dodgy as the turbulence was sloshing her around," said Brian. "We were quite relieved when we managed to use the lasso to get her out."

After rescuing the duck, workers named her "Lucky" and handed her over to the SSPCA, who returned her to the sea. "Lucky has now been released back beside her friends," an SSPCA spokeswoman said.

We adopted all three of our cats right from our own backyard! Pete belonged to someone else in the building who was ready to give him up. Lukie was one of several feral cats that we used to feed, and Joey came along and wandered into our back yard looking scruffy. Joey seemed to have no owner so we adopted him, too.

Prayer For All Animals

Dear Heavenly Father,

We come before You with praise and honor to ask for great blessings for all animals. May all of Your beautiful animal creatures praise Your Name! Guide and direct the hearts, minds, and spirits of good people everywhere to help animals who are in need.

We pray in the Name of Jesus that we would find great favor with You today that You would please:

Heal all animals from sickness and disease even as You declare in Isaiah 58:8, "then your light shall break forth like the dawn, and healing shall spring up quickly."

Pour out your blessings upon them that they will have long, healthy, and happy lives for the Glory of God. Let your angels watch over them, guide them, and keep them safe continually.

Remove all animals from the grasp of individuals who are currently abusing, neglecting, or harming them in any way. Disable all the powers of enemies that would come against them. Provide them with new homes and new caretakers that will shower them with love and affection and take wonderful care of them.

Shelter and hide them from evildoers and keep them out of harms way. Make them unavailable to any offenders and to those who would exploit, injure, harm or bring danger to them in any way. Psalm 91:3 says: "Surely He shall deliver thee from the snare of the fowler, and from the noisome pestilence."

Let all testing, studies, and experiments be done through computer technology, and in other ways that do not harm any lives, rather than through any animal testing. Put a great fear into evildoers everywhere that they will realize that they are accountable to You for any and all harm inflicted upon all of Your animals. **In Romans 14:12 it states, "so then every one of us shall give account of himself to God."**

Let all the animals find favor with You that every town, state, and community in the world will become "no-kill" animal communities. Grant that their fate will be according to Psalm 118:17, "I shall not die, but live, and declare the works of the Lord."

May all spay and neuter programs be very successful. We especially ask You to help all the feral cats that are not as fortunate as our own pets to have a good home. Please bless and help these cats and all the good people who are working on the spay, neuter and release programs for feral cats. Protect these little ones, and don't let anyone harm as much as a hair on their heads! Also, do not allow anyone to prohibit or interfere with the assistance and help that is being given to animals.

May every human being discover the truth from Your Word that there is eternal life for all animals in heaven, and respect Your creation. Give us the mind of Christ that we would think like you do toward every creature.

Teach people everywhere to value and respect all Your creatures. Help us to appreciate the wonderful gift of fellowship with our animal friends that You have given to us.

Bless each one with fresh food and water daily, and may their angels direct and guide them to safe places to stay. Put a hedge of safety around them at all times. For the Word of the Lord says in Psalm 4:8, "I will both lay me down in peace, and sleep: for Thou, Lord, only makest me dwell in safety."

Put a spirit of compassion and a desire to help and assist animals in need within the hearts of people everywhere. When we hear about any animal cruelty, please remind us to pray for the rescue, safety and protection of those animals. May You intercede on their behalf, Lord, and bring swift justice. Let us help out in any way that we can, such as signing petitions and letters that will help to enforce proper treatment of animals and punishment to the offenders.

We give You the praise, thanksgiving, honor and the glory in the Name of The Father, The Son, and The Holy Spirit. Amen.

He sendeth the springs into the valleys, which run among the hills. They give drink to every beast of the field: the wild asses quench their thirst. By them shall the fowls of the heaven have their habitation, which sing among the branches.

He watereth the hills from His chambers: the earth is satisfied with the fruit of Thy works. He causeth the grass to grow for the cattle, and herb for the service of man: that he may bring forth food out of the earth; And wine that maketh glad the heart of man, and oil to make his face to shine, and bread which strengtheneth man's heart.

The trees of the Lord are full of sap; the cedars of Lebanon, which He hath planted; Where the birds make their nests: as for the stork, the fir trees are her house. The high hills are a refuge for the wild goats; and the rocks for the conies.

He appointed the moon for seasons: the sun knoweth his going down. Thou makest darkness, and it is night: wherein all the beasts of the forest do creep forth.

The young lions roar after their prey, and seek their meat from God. The sun ariseth, they gather themselves together, and lay them down in their dens.

Psalm 104:10-22

Yea, the sparrow hath found a house, and the swallow a nest for herself, where she may lay her young, even Thine altars, O Lord of hosts, my King, and my God.

Psalm 84:3

If you have men who will exclude any of God's creatures from the shelter of compassion and pity, you will have men who will deal likewise with their fellow men.

Saint Francis of Assisi

I have compared thee, O my love,
to a company of horses in Pharaoh's chariots.

The Song of Solomon 1:9

Prayer for the Return of Lost Pets

I will instruct thee and teach thee
in the way which thou shalt go:
I will guide thee with Mine eye.

Psalm 32:8

There was a story in a newspaper called The Pilot, about a man from Sanford, North Carolina who has been very successful in finding lost pets by using his partner, Sabre, a red Doberman, to trace the pets' scent. The owner said, "usually what we do, is find an article the pet was sleeping with, chewing, whatever, to get the scent of the animal and pick it up. Then they leave from the pet's home to find the missing animal companion." The article said that Sabre has found most of the pets he has searched for, including 2 cats, 1 horse and 9 dogs.

Cat Found After 49 Days

Popcorn, a cat owned by Nancy, disappeared when her family moved from Oahu, Hawaii, to La Mesa, California. The cat was found seven weeks later in a cat carrier, elated to see her owners after having gone 49 days without food. This story is from Ripley's Believe It Or Not.

It is devastating to anyone who has a lost animal companion. Some common sense suggestions are to make sure you have an ID tag on your pet's collar with his/her name, your name and telephone number and address. They also have ID chips that you can use. One thing to keep in mind regarding the ID chips is that if you have only this, and do not have a collar with an ID tag, it will not be of any help to someone who takes in a stray pet and has no ability to read the chip. They may not ever take the pet to a vets office or shelter to find the identity through this chip. That's why I think all pets should wear a collar with a pet tag. We like to use breakaway collars. Make sure everyone in your household, as well as visitors, is aware

64

that your pet is not to be allowed outside. If you are having work done in your house or having something delivered and will need to keep the door open for any period of time, secure your pet in a closed room with water, food and a litter box.

When we were moving into our house we put Pete and Luke in one of the bedrooms and shut the door. There was a pet carrier in the room with the carrier door open in case one of them wanted to go back in it. One time when I was checking up on them to see how they were doing, I walked in and the both of them were jammed into one carrier together! The poor kids were really scared, and didn't quite understand that we were moving. It didn't take long after the activity and noise stopped and it became dark outside, that they ventured off into the house exploring their new home.

One day Lukie accidentally got outside. As I walked into the living room and looked toward the atrium doors, I was shocked to see Lukie standing on the wrong side of the door. He was outside on the deck looking at me through the door window! I prayed immediately, Lord, let him come right in safe and sound. I walked out on the deck and the basement door was open, which is how he got out, and I said, OK, let's go inside now and he was such a good boy and ran back in the house through the basement door.

When searching in your yard or near your home, you can try shaking a bag, box or the container of food that you normally use to feed them. Walk around shaking it while you call their name. The noise the food container makes is a familiar sound to them, and they will probably be hungry and may run back home to eat.

Bible Reading

> You have made known to me the path of life; You will fill me with joy in Your presence, with eternal pleasures at Your right hand.
>
> Psalm 16:11 NIV

From the end of the earth will I cry unto Thee, when my heart is overwhelmed: lead me to the rock that is higher than I. For Thou hast been a shelter for me, and a strong tower from the enemy.

Psalm 61:2-3

Here is a prayer to use to ask God to help you find your pet.

Prayer For The Return Of A Lost Pet

Dear Lord,

We ask You today to bring [name] back home to [his/her] family. We come before You to ask that we may find favor in Your sight today for the quick and safe return of [name]. We love [name] dearly and have great concerns regarding [his/her] safety. Guide our search effort and direct us to their location quickly. Please send Your angels out at this time and have them and the Holy Spirit guide [name] back home safe and sound. If anyone has [name] in their homes, we pray that You would arrange for their fast return to us. While [name] is on [her/his] way home to us, please keep [her/him] from all harm and danger. Allow no evil to befall them. As we recall in Your Word in Jeremiah 32:27, there isn't anything too hard for You to do. In Jesus Name we pray for the return of this precious animal companion. Thank You, Lord! Amen.

Amazing Grace, how sweet the sound,
That saved a wretch like me
I once was lost but now am found, was blind, but now, I see.
T'was Grace that taught my heart to fear.
And Grace, my fears relieved.
How precious did that Grace appear, the hour I first believed.
Through many dangers, toils and snares we have already come.
T'was Grace that brought us safe thus far,
and Grace will lead us home.

– From the Hymn "Amazing Grace" by John Newton

Prayer for Emergencies

I will both lay me down in peace, and sleep:
for Thou, Lord, only makest me dwell in safety.

Psalm 4:8

There are many constructive ways to prepare for any emergencies that may come up. One very important way is to pray to the Lord that He will watch over your beloved animal companions under every circumstance.

We've all heard the story about Scarlett, the mother cat from New York who saved her baby kittens from a burning building in 1996. Scarlet ran in and out of that burning building five times, until she got all her kittens out! She suffered burns on her face, back and feet and nearly lost her own life, but she was determined to save her babies. Here are some other heroic stories involving animals.

Collie Saves Owner's Life!

A collie named Jarrod in Hampstead, New Hampshire is credited with saving his owner's life. David said that Jarrod pushed him away from beneath his snow-covered roof and down a stairway seconds before the roof collapsed. "If I were under it I would have been crushed. The way I was leaning over the rail I would have been cut in half, I would have been killed," said David. The weight of the 12-by-14-foot roof was later estimated at nearly 4,000 pounds.

David, 61, is disabled by severe arthritis and spinal problems and uses crutches. He believes his 1-½ year old collie, who is trained to help him get around in his wheelchair, knew exactly what he was doing and saved his life.

Doesn't it make you wonder how Jarrod knew that the roof was about to cave in? The intelligence of animals is incredible as we have seen from these stories and what boggles the mind in this story is not only the dog's intelligence and thought process, but also his planning to prevent a disaster from taking place. I believe animals can see many things in the spiritual world that we cannot.

'Miracle Dog' Sparks Awareness Campaign

His name is Quentin, and he's one lucky dog. Not many would have thought so after Quentin, a 30-pound Besenji mix entered a St. Louis gas chamber, which was packed with unwanted dogs. But when the death chamber doors opened again, Quentin greeted animal-control supervisor Rosemary with his tail and tongue wagging. Quentin – named for the San Quentin State Prison – beat the odds, and so Rosemary didn't have the heart to put him back into the gas chamber.

Instead, she turned him over to Randy, the founder of Stray Rescue of St. Louis. Randy said that Quentin's "bad days are behind him for good." And with that thought in mind, Randy took Quentin's story public. "To me, it's a miracle or divine intervention," Randy said. "I can't help but think he's here to serve a higher purpose." Randy felt his thoughts were confirmed when In Defense of Animals, a Mill Valley, California-based organization, asked Randy if Quentin could be their "spokesdog" in their campaign to educate the public about the plight of millions of dogs facing euthanasia. About 5 million dogs are euthanized each year because no one is willing to adopt them, In Defense of Animals founder, Elliot, said. The American Society for the Prevention of Cruelty to Animals estimates that between 5 and 9 million companion animals are euthanized each year.

Two days after his ordeal, Randy said that Quentin was a little malnourished but "in very good condition." They found a good home for Quentin and now he's a blessing to his new family.

Abraham Lincoln Rescued Birds

Once, while riding through the country with some other lawyers, Lincoln was missed from the party, and was seen loitering near a thicket of wild plum trees where the men had stopped a short time before to water their horses. "Where is Lincoln?" asked one of the lawyers. "When I saw him last," answered another, "he had caught two young birds that the wind had blown out of their nest, and was hunting for the nest to put them back again."

As Lincoln joined them, the lawyers teased him on his tender-heartedness, and he said: — "I could not have slept unless I had restored those little birds to their mother." Lincoln had several pets. He had a turkey named Jack, two goats named Nanny and Nanko, ponies, cats, dogs, pigs and a white rabbit. Another interesting fact about Abraham Lincoln was that he used to spend one hour each morning reading the Bible!

(By Noah Brooks – Adapted.)

Dolphins Protect Swimmers From Shark

In Wellington, New Zealand a pod of dolphins circled protectively round a group of New Zealand swimmers to fend off an attack by a great white shark. Lifesavers

Rob, his daughters Niccy, Karina and Helen were swimming 300 feet off Ocean Beach near Whangarei on New Zealand's North Island when the dolphins herded them — apparently to protect them from a shark. "They started to herd us up, they pushed all four of us together by doing tight circles around us," Rob told the New Zealand Press Association (NZPA).

Rob tried to drift away from the group, but two of the bigger dolphins herded him back just as he spotted a 9-foot great white shark swimming towards the group. "I just recoiled. It was only about 2 meters (6 feet) away from me, the water was crystal clear and it was as clear as the nose on my face," Rob said. "They had corralled us up to protect us," he said. The lifesavers spent the next 40 minutes surrounded by the dolphins before they could safely swim back to shore.

Prayer For Emergencies

Dear Heavenly Father,

We ask that You would continually watch over [name] and intercede for [her/his] protection. Should there be any imminent danger, please provide a quick route of escape for [her/his] total safety, and ours. Thank you for all the angels that you have assigned to take care of us and for all Your Blessings. We ask in Jesus Name, Amen.

Our soul is escaped as a bird
out of the snare of the fowlers:
the snare is broken, and we are escaped.
Our help is in the Name of the Lord,
Who made heaven and earth.

Psalm 124:7-8

Safety On the Roads

For every beast of the forest is Mine,
and the cattle upon a thousand hills.
I know all the fowls of the mountains:
and the wild beasts of the field are Mine.

Psalm 50:10-11

Praying Before We Travel

Peter Hammond, Director of Frontline Fellowship says, "I regularly pray before every mission trip that no animal will be hurt by my vehicle. I've had numerous close calls, but by God's grace, the Lord has protected me from injuring any animals during the hundreds of thousands of kilometers driven by vehicle and off road motorbike over some of the worst roads in Africa."

Prayer For Protection While Traveling

Dear Lord,

Please put it on the hearts and minds of people driving automobiles to be careful when any animals are present. We ask for your protection for all animals, both pets that may find themselves outdoors, and all wildlife. Lead and guide them to keep off of the roadways when vehicles are present. Instill in their minds that they should wait until all is quiet and safe before they venture out into the streets and roads. May your angels keep them out of harms way. Your Word says that You are a present help in time of trouble (Psalm 46:1), and we ask that You would protect them at the present time that they require it. Thank you for Your blessings. In Jesus Name, Amen.

My help comes from the Lord,
the Maker of heaven and earth.

Psalm 121:2 NIV

Prayer for Pet Shelters

Thou openest Thine hand,
and satisfieth the desire of every living thing.

Psalm 145:16

The Ark Shelter in South Carolina

We can help pets in shelters by praying, donating money, time, supplies and services. Some people provide foster homes for shelter pets when they become too full. One of the wonderful and genuine qualities of people who help animals is that they do it completely from their hearts. An animal can't repay us in a monetary way or by doing us a favor. Anyone who has ever owned a pet knows, of course, that animals give to us in ways that cannot be fully communicated. Their love, companionship, and loyalty far exceed that of many people and is priceless!

Here are some Bible verses about helping animals and people in need.

Bible Readings

Give, and it will be given to you. A good measure, pressed down, shaken together and running over, will be poured into your lap. For with the measure you use, it will be measured to you.

Luke 6:38 NIV

In everything I did, I showed you that by this kind of hard work we must help the weak, remembering the words the Lord Jesus Himself said: 'It is more blessed to give than to receive.'

Acts 20:35 NIV

Remember this: Whoever sows sparingly will also reap sparingly, and whoever sows generously will also reap generously.

II Corinthians 9:6 NIV

Blessed is he who has regard for the weak; the Lord delivers him in times of trouble.

Psalm 41:1 NIV

And if you spend yourselves in behalf of the hungry and satisfy the needs of the oppressed, then your light will rise in the darkness, and your night will become like the noonday.

Isaiah 58:10 NIV

He who gives to the poor will lack nothing, but he who closes his eyes to them receives many curses.

Proverbs 28:27 NIV

He who is kind to the poor lends to the Lord, and He . will reward him for what he has done.

Proverbs 19:17 NIV

Then the King will say to those on His right, 'Come, you who are blessed by My Father; take your inheritance, the kingdom prepared for you since the creation of the world. For I was hungry and you gave Me something to eat, I was thirsty and you gave Me something to drink, I was a stranger and you invited Me in, I needed clothes and you clothed Me, I was sick and you looked after Me, I was in prison and you came to visit Me.'

Then the righteous will answer Him, "Lord, when did we see You hungry and feed You, or thirsty and give You something to drink? When did we see You a stranger and invite You in, or needing clothes and clothe You? When did we see You sick or in prison and go to visit You?" The King will reply, "I tell you the truth, whatever you did for one of the least of these brothers of Mine, you did for Me."

Matthew 25:34-40 NIV

Prayer For Animal Shelters

Heavenly Father,

We ask in Jesus' Name that You would pour out Your blessings upon all the animal shelters everywhere. May every worker take special care of these creatures the same way they would want to be taken care of themselves. Let all shelters become no-kill shelters for the Glory of God. For we know that You did not create these animals so that people would kill them, but rather that they would have life and more abundantly. Please provide adequate funding and provisions for these shelters.

May they have ample food, water, litter, medical treatment, and all the other supplies they have need of. Give shelter operators a spirit of discernment to know who should adopt the animals, and deny anyone who does not meet God's standards for caring for the pets.

May only good, loving, and caring individuals who will do their best to give them the longest, healthiest, and happiest life possible adopt them. We ask You to bless every animal in every shelter.

Heal them of any sicknesses they may have. We pray that these little ones will find favor with You, that You would provide them with all their needs, and establish them in a home with a loving family.

Put it in the hearts and minds of people everywhere to give finances, time, love, and supplies because Your Word teaches us that it is more blessed to give than to receive (Acts 20:35). Amen.

I care not for a man's religion
whose dog and cat are not the better for it.

Abraham Lincoln

Lena, from Canada

Prayer for Tough Laws Against Animal Cruelty

A righteous man regardeth the life of his beast;
but the tender mercies of the wicked are cruel.

Proverbs 12:10

Remember to sign petitions for the protection of animals. Also, if we are asked to vote on laws protecting the animals, we should do so. We can pray and have faith, but the Bible says that faith without works or deeds is dead (James 2:26). In other words, take action and do something positive.

Bible Readings

Break the arm of the wicked and evil man; call him to account for his wickedness that would not be found out.

Psalm 10:15

Rise up, O God, and defend Your cause; remember how fools mock You all day long. Do not ignore the clamor of Your adversaries, the uproar of Your enemies, which rises continually.

Psalm 74:22-23

Prayer To End Animal Cruelty

We pray that every individual and lawmaker would become heightened to the importance of tough and enforceable laws against animal abusers. May the laws become as strict as they are for human beings. Open the eyes of every lawmaker and citizen and those in a position to enforce these changes, to see clearly that there is a direct connection between cruelty to animals and cruelty to people. Please help us to pass laws that will protect Your beautiful creatures everywhere. Your Word says in Psalm 91:3: Surely He shall deliver thee from the snare of the fowler, and from the noisome pestilence. We pray that you would rescue all the animals out of the snare of the wicked ones, and deliver them from all evil (Matthew 7:13). Amen.

Chapter 5

Blessing The Animals

The first week in October is traditionally recognized as a time to remember the legacy of Saint Francis of Assisi, and his great love for all animals. There are many services that take place to bless and honor our beautiful animal companions. You can conduct your own service as often as you wish, and perhaps get together with fellow pet parents, and have your own service. For song suggestions, see the Bibliography section.

The Blessing of the Animals Service in this chapter has been created to assist you with your own services. You can edit the service to suit your own preferences. You can read these stories or add your own. Perhaps there's an interesting story about one of the pets in your own Blessing of the Animals service. A blessing service is a tangible extension of the love and peace that we share with all God's creatures.

The Blessing of the Animals Service

St. Francis of Assisi inspired the Blessing of the Animals service. St. Francis of Assisi (1182-1226), Patron Saint of Animals and Ecology, preached the gospel to the birds, rabbits, wolves, and all creatures. He called them "brother" and "sister." He gave them his blessing. Within the Blessing of the Animals service you'll find one of the stories told about St. Francis, which was first recorded by Thomas of Celano during the 13th century.

Animals are not only a blessing to us, but here are a couple of stories about animals and people who were a great blessing to each other.

Cat Saves Lamb

A lamb that escaped recently from his pasture in England was saved from drowning in a swimming pool by an alert cat. Puss Puss, a black and white cat, discovered the lamb's predicament and frantically meowed, running back and forth between the pool and the garden where her owners were working, to alert them to his plight.

Puss Puss's owners were gardeners who had taken her along with them to work at the garden of Cotswold District Council in Icomb, Cheltenham. They found the cat was in a very, very agitated state, meowing, calling, crying, and being an utter pest. She was dashing back and forward between them and the pool. Finally, they went to the pool, and they found the lamb in the swimming pool and got him out quickly and the lamb was all right.

When they found the lamb he was under the pool cover and his head was entangled in the pool cover straps, which actually were keeping him from drowning. They jumped into the pool to rescue the lamb. Puss Puss was a real little superstar! The actions of the quick-thinking feline are all the more remarkable, because she is disabled. As a kitten she had an accident, and had to have her tail amputated. She didn't grow properly, has arthritis and can't curl up, jump or climb like other normal cats. Puss Puss is truly a remarkable creature.

A Girl Wants To Save A Sick Giraffe

Nine-year-old Autumn wanted only one thing for Christmas. She wanted to help and meet Beau, a giraffe from the Franklin Park Zoo, Boston, Massachusetts. Autumn raised more than $1,100 for Beau who was stricken with an incurable disease. Peracute mortality syndrome is an affliction whose cause is unknown and results in severe malnutrition typically followed by death.

Autumn, a self-proclaimed lover of all four-legged creatures, learned of Beau's plight. The image of the skinny giraffe, 300 pounds underweight, stuck in her mind. She said, "Mommy, I want to help that giraffe." She sprang into action. Instead of playing at recess, she collected coins from her pals. Instead of cashing in birthday checks, Autumn stuffed the money into a canister for Beau's fund, and persuaded her parents to set up a collection can for Beau in their convenience store.

Her father wrote a letter to the zoo. "There's not too many 9-year-olds who are willing to give up Christmas presents to meet a giraffe," he said. "So I had to make her dreams come true." The zookeepers were happy to fulfill Autumn's wish. They drove her and her family directly to the pen where Beau lives.

The zookeepers began feeding him a special blend of fresh green leaves, branches, and vegetables that must be imported from warmer climates during the cold Massachusetts winter. It's an expensive diet – $50,000 a year, but it seems to be paying off. Beau is around his normal weight now, 1600 pounds, but zookeepers closely monitor him in hope of preventing a sudden relapse. This story appeared in The Boston Globe.

You can anoint the pet's forehead with a little oil, which represents the Holy Spirit.

Prayer For A Blessing Of The Animals Service

Dear Lord,

Your Word says "I was glad when they said unto me, let us go into the house of the Lord" (Psalm 122:1). Thank You for this day that You have given us. We know that You delight in all Your creatures, and that You are the giver of all life and of all blessings. You created the animals and said, "It is good."

Bless each animal here today, and those who could not attend. We thank You Lord Jesus that John 10:10 says that You have come that we would have life and more abundantly. You also said that by Me thy days shall be multiplied, and the years of thy life shall be increased (Proverbs 9:11). Thank You for a long, healthy, and happy life for each animal companion. Praise God for their good health. We recall that the Bible says bless the Lord, O my soul, and forget not all His promises, Who heals all your diseases (Psalm 103:2-3).

We praise God that You are faithful and keep them from evil (II Thes. 3:3). We ask that You would provide for their every need, keep them safe, healthy, happy, and give them exceedingly long lives for the Glory of God. In the Name of the Father, the Son and the Holy Spirit, Amen.

Bible Readings

And God said, "Let the land produce living creatures according to their kinds: livestock, creatures that move along the ground, and wild animals, each according to its kind." And it was so. God made the wild animals according to their kinds, the livestock according to their kinds, and all the creatures that move along the ground according to their kinds. And God saw that it was good.

Genesis 1:24-25 NIV

Did you know that God made a covenant with the animals? After the flood, Noah, his family, and all the animals entered into a covenant with God. This covenant was not only made with Noah and his family, but God repeatedly states that He is entering into a covenant with the animals. The covenant states that God will never again cut off all life with a flood. These scriptures are where the term "rainbow bridge" comes from.

"I now establish My covenant with you and with your descendants after you and with every living creature that was with you – the birds, the livestock and all the wild animals, all those that came out of the ark with you – every living creature on earth. I establish My covenant with you: Never again will all life be cut off by the waters of a flood; never again will there be a flood to destroy the earth."

And God said, "This is the sign of the covenant I am making between Me and you and every living creature with you, a covenant for all generations to come: I have set My rainbow in the clouds, and it will be the sign of the covenant between Me and the earth.

Whenever I bring clouds over the earth and the rainbow appears in the clouds, I will remember my covenant between Me and you and all living creatures of every kind. Never again will the waters become a flood to destroy all life. Whenever the rainbow appears in the clouds, I will see it and remember the everlasting covenant between God and all living creatures of every kind on the earth."

So God said to Noah, "This is the sign of the covenant I have established between me and all life on the earth."

Genesis 9:9-17 NIV

God commanded the Israelites to take one day a week off from work, and this included the animals, as you'll see in this next verse.

Six days you shall labor and do all your work, but the seventh day is a Sabbath to the Lord your God. On it you shall not do any work, neither you, nor your son or daughter, nor your manservant or maidservant, nor your animals, nor the alien within your gates.

Exodus 20:9-10 NIV

Thou art worthy, O Lord, to receive glory and honour and power: for Thou hast created all things and for Thy pleasure they are and were created.

Revelation 4:11

We give thanks to God always for you all, making mention of you in our prayers.

I Thessalonians 1:2

Grace be unto you, and peace, from God our Father, and from the Lord Jesus Christ.

Philippians 1:2

A Story About St. Francis of Assisi

Father Francis and his companions were making a trip through the Spoleto Valley near the town of Bevagna. Suddenly, Francis spotted a great number of birds of all varieties. There were doves, crows and all sorts of birds. Swept up in the moment, Francis left his friends in the road and ran after the birds, who patiently waited for him. He greeted them in his usual way, expecting them to scurry off into the air as he spoke. But they moved not.

Filled with awe, he asked them if they would stay awhile and listen to the Word of God. He said to them: "My brother and sister birds, you should praise your

Creator and always love Him: He gave you feathers for clothes, wings to fly and all other things that you need. It is God who made you noble among all creatures, making your home in thin, pure air. Without sowing or reaping, you receive God's guidance and protection."

At this the birds began to spread their wings, stretch their necks and gaze at Francis, rejoicing and praising God in a wonderful way according to their nature. Francis then walked right through the middle of them, turned around and came back, touching their heads and bodies with his tunic.

Then he gave them his blessing, making the sign of the cross over them. At that they flew off and Francis, rejoicing and giving thanks to God, went on his way.

St. Francis seemed to emphasize the viewpoint that all creatures make up one family of creation under one loving Creator in heaven. We form one community – one symphony of praise – with our brother and sister creatures.

Bible Reading

The Lord is my shepherd; I shall not want. He maketh me to lie down in green pastures: He leadeth me beside the still waters. He restoreth my soul: He leadeth me in the paths of righteousness for His name's sake.

Yea, though I walk through the valley of the shadow of death, I will fear no evil: for Thou art with me; Thy rod and Thy staff they comfort me. Thou preparest a table before me in the presence of mine enemies: Thou anointest my head with oil; my cup runneth over. Surely goodness and mercy shall follow me all the days of my life: and I will dwell in the house of the Lord for ever.

Psalm Chapter 23

Blessing Of The Animals – Closing Prayer

The Lord bless you and keep you; the Lord make His face shine upon you and be gracious to you; the Lord turn His face toward you and give you peace. Amen. (Numbers 6:24-26 NIV).

Janis Nedelec's cat, Maui

Chapter 6

Blessings For All Occasions

Thanksgiving Blessings

Give thanks to the Lord, for He is good;
His love endures forever.

Psalm 118:1 NIV

We give God thanks every day, and especially at Thanksgiving for our beautiful animal companions, as well as our other family members, our homes, food, health, and our lives. Psalm 100:1-2 says we should make a joyful shout to the Lord, and serve Him with gladness. We should come into His presence with singing. Here are some stories about Thanksgiving and sharing food that I think you'll like.

THOMAS HENRY AND MARY ANN.

Cat and Turtle Share A Saucer Of Milk

In Rev. J. G. Wood's book *Petland* dated 1890 he wrote of a cat named Thomas Henry who was a real darling. The family also had a turtle named Mary Ann. Thomas Henry was devoted to her. They used to drink milk out of the same saucer, and when they had finished, Thomas Henry would lick the milk off Mary Ann's head and neck, and tidy her up.

Maui, Janis Nedelec's cat

Cat Sneaks Into House On Thanksgiving

One Thanksgiving Day Niki's mother was cooking in her house, and it began to get too hot in the kitchen. She opened the storm door a few inches to let some air in, and continued with her meal preparation.

All the family assembled and had a lovely Thanksgiving dinner, dessert and time together. After all the family had left, her mother was doing some last minute clean-up in the kitchen when out walked a strange cat from the back bedroom, which was formerly Niki's bedroom. He then departed out of the same door that he had come in through. Niki's mother was quite startled to see the feline, as she had no idea that the cat ever came into the house. It seems that the food smelled so good in her kitchen that the cat decided to come in.

However, with all the commotion of the guests and the activity in the house, the cat must have been too scared to come out until it was quiet again.

We were all surprised and amused when my mother told us about our secret guest that Thanksgiving Day.

Unfortunately, the cat never had a chance to taste any of the food that smelled so good.

Birds Eat Berries

Rev. J. G. Wood wrote that around 1871 one of his friends near Manchester, England had a garden with a very fine mountain-ash tree, which always produced a plentiful crop of berries. Shortly before the fruit ripened, a great number of birds got together at the end of the garden, and were very noisy, chattering and evidently discussing some subject on which they were not agreed.

This went on for days while the berries were ripening. Then one morning an order appeared to be issued, the birds flew to the tree, and in a couple of hours there was not a berry left on it. This occurred regularly during the three years that Wood's friend owned the property. This story is from *Man and Beast: Here and Hereafter* by Rev. J. G. Wood.

Thanksgiving Blessing Prayer

Dear Heavenly Father,

We come before You today with a heart full of thanksgiving for the beautiful creatures that you have provided for our companionship, love, joy and happiness.

Thank you for the sweet songs of the birds. Thank you for blessing our animal companions, and so wonderfully providing the gift of eternal life for them in heaven with us. In Philippians 4:6 we learn that in everything, by prayer and petition, with thanksgiving, we should present our requests to God. We ask You for lifelong blessings of joy, good health, and great happiness for our animal companions.

We ask that You would please bless [name] in the Name of the Father, the Son and the Holy Spirit. May You provide them with a very long, healthy, and happy life with us. Keep them out of harms way always. Amen.

Bible Readings

Give, and it will be given to you. A good measure, pressed down, shaken together and running over, will be poured into your lap. For with the measure you use, it will be measured to you.

Luke 6:38 NIV

The Lord is good to all: and His tender mercies are over all His works.

Psalm 145:9

Sing unto the Lord with the harp; with the harp, and the voice of a psalm. With trumpets and sound of cornet make a joyful noise before the Lord, the King. Let the sea roar, and the fullness thereof; the world, and they that dwell therein. Let the floods clap their hands: let the hills be joyful together. Before the Lord; for He cometh to judge the earth: with righteousness shall He judge the world, and the people with equity.

Psalm 98:5-9

I will extol Thee, my God, O king; and I will bless Thy name for ever and ever. Every day will I bless Thee; and I will praise Thy name for ever and ever. Great is the Lord, and greatly to be praised; and His greatness is unsearchable.

One generation shall praise Thy works to another, and shall declare Thy mighty acts. I will speak of the glorious honour of Thy majesty, and of Thy wondrous works.

Psalm 145:1-5

All creatures of our God and King,
Lift up your voice and with us sing;
Alleluia! Alleluia!
Thou burning sun with golden beam,
Thou silver moon with softer gleam!
O praise Him, O praise Him!
Alleluia! Alleluia!

Saint Francis of Assisi, 1182-1226
– From the Hymn "All Creatures Of Our God And King"

Easter

There is a green hill far away
Without the city wall,
Where the dear Lord was crucified,
Who died to save us all.
There was no other good enough
To pay the price of sin:
He only could unlock the gate
Of heaven, and let us in.

C. F. Alexander

We are most fortunate creatures that because of Jesus' death and resurrection, we are able to be reconciled with God and enjoy eternal life. At Easter time one of the things that often comes to mind is the donkey that Jesus rode on. I've taken a photo of a donkey to show you the cross that's formed along their spine and across their shoulders.

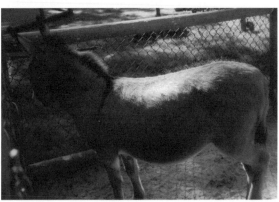

How The Donkey Got Its Cross

The markings on many donkeys consist of one long dark line along their spine and a shorter dark line across their shoulders, which form a cross. There's an old legend that donkeys have that cross because a donkey carried Jesus to His birth and carried Him on Palm Sunday. The donkey regularly appears in the nativity scene, and its presence at the birth of Jesus suggests that even the humblest of animals could recognize the new Son of God. Jesus rode a donkey, which nobody had ever ridden before when He went to the cross to die for the world.

> As He approached Bethphage and Bethany at the hill called the Mount of Olives, He sent two of His disciples, saying to them, "Go to the village ahead of you, and as you enter it, you will find a colt tied there, which no one has ever ridden. Untie it and bring it here. If anyone asks you, 'Why are you untying it?' tell him, 'The Lord needs it.'" Those who were sent ahead went and found it just as He had told them.

Luke 19-29-32 NIV

Photo of Tiggy and her new family

Tiggy's Easter Story

One day Dave, Janis Nedelec's husband, noticed a homeless cat living underneath his trailer at his construction site in downtown Vancouver. He would only get quick glimpses of the cat now and then, as it would not let itself be seen by anyone. Dave prepared a covered area with an animal carrier he brought from home and put a blanket in it. Of course, he supplied this cat with food and fresh water daily. He named the cat 'Smoke' because it was gray.

Janis urged him to try to befriend it so he could catch it, and at the very least take it to the SPCA because they couldn't take in another cat. But he and others at the construction site had been unable to get near the cat let alone catch it.

Dave asked around to see if anyone would want the cat in case he was able to catch it. However, no one wanted a cat. So Janis started to pray fervently for this precious little animal that it would become friendly and allow someone to catch it, but to no avail. Meanwhile, Dave would report to Janis that every time he did see Smoke, he seemed to be getting bigger and bigger, fatter and fatter. He wondered if it was getting fed too much or if it might be pregnant.

Nothing happened until around the end of March when Shaun, a nice fellow who loves cats, came to work on the construction site. He came to know about the cat and he tried to befriend it, but to no avail either. Finally on Good Friday, which was his day off, Shaun decided to borrow a trap from the SPCA and try to trap it. Janis prayed and prayed that day that he would be successful as she really wanted to see that little kitty have a loving home.

Well, he did catch Smoke and he brought her home and provided a secluded area to start off with in a room in his house. This nice fellow changed Smoke's name to Tiggy. He had two other cats so he would have to break them all in slowly. Shaun did a wonderful job of it. He kept them separated at first. He let them look at each other through a screen on the door.

Now this is not the end of the story. Three days later on Easter Monday in the wee hours of the morning Tiggy started giving birth! She is now the proud mother of seven precious little kitties. She has become tame, and has befriended Shaun and his cats very nicely. Shaun found homes for all of Tiggy's kittens, but kept one of them as well as Tiggy. Shaun and his cats are one happy family. It's an answer to prayer. You know Easter is a time of celebrating life, and this certainly is the story of one cat and her kitten's new lives, isn't it? Thank you, Lord!

Janis Nedelec, our prayer partner
From British Columbia, Canada

What means this eager, anxious throng –
Which moves with busy haste along,
These wondrous gatherings day by day –
What means this great commotion, pray?
In accents hushed the throng reply,
"Jesus of Nazareth passeth by."

Emma Campbell

Easter Blessing Prayer

Grace be unto you, and peace, from God our Father, and from the Lord Jesus Christ. We thank You heavenly Father for sending Your Son, Jesus Christ, to live among us, as God in the flesh. Greater love hath no man than this, that He lay down His life for His friends. Thank you for His resurrection that has made it possible for every one of Your creatures to share in eternal life.

We pray for a special blessing to be upon our animal companions, and all the animals of the world. Now the grace of our Lord Jesus Christ, who lives and reigns with God the Father, be with you and your families. Amen.

Bible Readings

For since by man came death, by man came also the resurrection of the dead.

I Corinthians 15:21

Greater love hath no man than this, that a man lay down His life for His friends.

John 15:13

After the Sabbath, at dawn on the first day of the week, Mary Magdalene and the other Mary went to look at the tomb. There was a violent earthquake, for an angel of the Lord came down from heaven and, going to the tomb, rolled back the stone and sat on it. His appearance was like lightning, and His clothes were white as snow. The guards were so afraid of Him that they shook and became like dead men.

The angel said to the women, "Do not be afraid, for I know that you are looking for Jesus, who was crucified. He is not here; He has risen, just as He said. Come and see the place where He lay. Then go quickly and tell His disciples: 'He has risen from the dead and is going ahead of you into Galilee. There you will see Him.' Now I have told you."

So the women hurried away from the tomb, afraid yet filled with joy, and ran to tell His disciples. Suddenly Jesus met them. "Greetings," He said. They came to Him, clasped His feet and worshiped Him. Then Jesus said to them, "Do not be afraid. Go and tell My brothers to go to Galilee; there they will see Me."

Matthew 28:1-10 NIV

The Lord Is My Shepherd

The Lord is my shepherd; I shall not want. He maketh me to lie down in green pastures: He leadeth me beside the still waters. He restoreth my soul: He leadeth me in the paths of righteousness for His Name's sake.

Yea, though I walk through the valley of the shadow of death, I will fear no evil: for Thou art with me; Thy rod and Thy staff they comfort me. Thou preparest a table before me in the presence of mine enemies: Thou

anointest my head with oil; my cup runneth over.
Surely goodness and mercy shall follow me all the days
of my life: and I will dwell in the house of the Lord for
ever.

Psalm Chapter 23

The Lamb

Little Lamb, who made thee?
Dost thou know who made thee?
Gave thee life, and bid thee feed
By the stream and o'er the mead;
Gave thee clothing of delight,
Softest clothing, woolly, bright;
Gave thee such a tender voice,
Making all the vales rejoice?
Little Lamb, who made thee?
Dost thou know who made thee?

Little Lamb, I'll tell thee,
Little Lamb, I'll tell thee:
He is called by thy name,
For He calls Himself a Lamb.
He is meek, and He is mild;
He became a little child.
I a child, and thou a lamb.
We are called by His name.
Little Lamb, God bless thee!
Little Lamb, God bless thee!

– William Blake, 1757-1827

Christmas

After they had heard the king, they went on their way,
and the star they had seen in the east went ahead of them
until it stopped over the place where the Child was.
When they saw the star, they were overjoyed.
On coming to the house, they saw the Child
with His mother Mary, and they bowed down
and worshiped Him. Then they opened their
treasures and presented Him with
gifts of gold and of incense and of myrrh.

Matthew 2:9-11 NIV

Pete and Luke Shanahan

Pete Always Loved Christmas

Our cat, Pete, who now lives in heaven, always loved
Christmas and especially his Christmas tree every year.
He couldn't wait for us to buy the tree and bring it in
the house. Before we could even set it up, he would be
sitting under "his" Christmas tree ready to celebrate the
holidays. He loved the smell of the tree, and had lots of
fun opening all his presents. He used to exchange gifts
with his grandma and auntie for years. You would
frequently find him camped out under his tree during
the holiday season.

Pete under his Christmas tree

The Boy That Gave His Cow Money To God

At Christmas we think about the three wise men who came to Jesus bearing gifts and that's why we like to give gifts at Christmas. There was a 12-year-old boy who gave a special gift once to God's work. He was in a church service, and he went up and gave an offering of $5.00.

He was crying and the pastor wanted to know why he was crying. The boy said, "that's my cow money in there." He told him that he had always wanted a cow of his own. His Dad had told him that they were going to live in a place where he would be able to have a cow, but he'd have to pay for it. He had been saving up for nine months doing errands and taking a paper route. The pastor asked him why he was putting the cow money in the offering. He said, because God told me to. The pastor said, "How do you know God told you

97

to?" The boy said, "I heard Him and I know it was God and He called me by my name."

When the pastor told the congregation about the boy's great sacrifice, a big man with bib overalls walked up front and said, "God told me to give this boy a cow." The pastor said, "You have a cow?" He said, "I have thousands of them." It turned out that he was the biggest rancher in the state of Washington. He did give the boy a cow, and the boy selected the best one, too! When God told the boy to give up his cow money, He already had a cow waiting for him! This boy's act of obedience pleased God, and He rewarded him for it! This story was taken from the book *Miracles, Greater Miracles* by R. W. Schambach.

Gift Giving By President Ronald Reagan

During Ronald Reagan's presidency he would collect acorns when he went to Camp David. He kept the acorns in his desk drawer, and the squirrels would sit outside the Oval Office waiting for a handout.

Some squirrels would eat the acorns right out of President Reagan's hand! Ronald Reagan's pets included a spaniel named Rex and a sheepdog named Lucky. From Animal People newspaper, June 2004.

A Christmas Prayer

Unto Thee, Father, we lift up our eyes, Thou that dwells in the heavens. We thank You for Your precious Son who became a tiny baby in a stable in Bethlehem in simplicity. He has changed our world and our lives for the better for evermore. May Your light illuminate our hearts and may the hope, peace, joy and love represented by the birth in Bethlehem fill our lives, and become a part of us. Jesus, the light of the world, we celebrate Your birth today. Let us show the love and kindness of God in our lives, and may we be a special blessing to You, Lord, everyday. In Jesus Name we pray. Amen.

The Prophecy of Jesus by Isaiah

For unto us a Child is born, unto us a Son is given: and the government shall be upon His shoulder: and His name shall be called Wonderful, Counsellor, The mighty God, The everlasting Father, The Prince of Peace. Of the increase of His government and peace there shall be no end, upon the throne of David, and upon His kingdom, to order it, and to establish it with judgment and with justice from henceforth even for ever. The zeal of the Lord of hosts will perform this.

Isaiah 9:6-7

The Birth of Jesus

And it came to pass in those days, that there went out a decree from Caesar Augustus that all the world should be taxed. (And this taxing was first made when Cyrenius was governor of Syria.) And all went to be taxed, every one into his own city. And Joseph also went up from Galilee, out of the city of Nazareth, into Judaea, unto the city of David, which is called Bethlehem; (because he was of the house and lineage of David:) to be taxed with Mary his espoused wife, being great with child.

And so it was, that, while they were there, the days were accomplished that she should be delivered. And she brought forth her firstborn Son, and wrapped Him in swaddling clothes, and laid Him in a manger; because there was no room for them in the inn. And there were in the same country shepherds abiding in the field, keeping watch over their flock by night. And, lo, the angel of the Lord came upon them, and the glory of the Lord shone round about them: and they were sore afraid. And the angel said unto them, Fear not: for, behold, I bring you good tidings of great joy, which shall be to all people.

For unto you is born this day in the city of David a Saviour, which is Christ the Lord. And this shall be a sign unto you; Ye shall find the Babe wrapped in swaddling clothes, lying in a manger.

And suddenly there was with the angel a multitude of the heavenly host praising God, and saying, Glory to God in the highest, and on earth peace, good will toward men.

And it came to pass, as the angels were gone away from them into heaven, the shepherds said one to another, Let us now go even unto Bethlehem, and see this thing which is come to pass, which the Lord hath made known unto us. And they came with haste, and found Mary, and Joseph, and the Babe lying in a manger.

Luke 2:1-16

Cappy, my aunt's dog

Valentine's Day

So love in our hearts shall grow mighty and strong.
Through crosses, through sorrows, through manifold wrong.

H. W. Longfellow

On Valentine's Day we show our love for one another. Here is a story of a special love and bond that a cat and dog once had for each other. It's from Rev. J. G. Wood's book called ***Man and Beast: Here and Hereafter***. This anecdote shows that animals belonging to different species, such as the dog and cat, can communicate ideas to each other, and act in concert. It also shows their great love and devotion to one another.

Cat And Dog Teamwork

A relation of mine in Dumfries-shire had a dog and a cat, which were attached to each other in an extraordinary manner, and both were great favorites in the household. The dog, however, was not intended to sleep in the house, and was carefully put out every night; but, strange to say, he was always found in the morning lying before the fire, with the cat by his side.

One evening, the master of the dog heard a sort of rap at a back door leading to the kitchen, and saw the shrewd cat spring up and strike the latch, while the dog pushed open the door and entered in triumph. This system must have long been carried on, and when it was discovered, I need not say how interested were the members of the household in these intelligent and really wonderful creatures.

Kangaroo Saves Owner

A farmer who suffered serious head injuries after being struck by a falling tree branch was rescued by a partially blind kangaroo who is being hailed as a hero. Lulu the kangaroo banged on the door of the family's home in Morwell, Gippsland in southeast Australia after discovering the farmer lying unconscious in a field.

According to a Rural Ambulance Victoria paramedic named Eddie, the man had been checking his property for damage following a severe storm when he was struck by the branch. Eddie said that if Len's family had not found him so quickly, he might have died. "The kangaroo alerted them to where he was and went and sat down next to him, and that's how they found him," he said.

Len was taken to an Austin hospital. Len's daughter Celeste said, "Lulu and Dad are very close and she follows him around, but we all just love her so much." About ten years ago, the family found Lulu in the pouch of her mother who had been killed by a car. The authorities allowed them to care for Lulu and adopt her because she is missing one eye. The Australian Royal

Society for the Prevention of Cruelty to Animals (RSPCA) has urged the family to nominate Lulu for its National Bravery Award.

Bible Readings

God's Love And Ours

Dear friends, let us love one another, for love comes from God. Everyone who loves has been born of God and knows God. Whoever does not love does not know God, because God is love. This is how God showed His love among us: He sent His one and only Son into the world that we might live through Him. This is love: not that we loved God, but that He loved us and sent His Son as an atoning sacrifice for our sins.

Dear friends, since God so loved us, we also ought to love one another. No one has ever seen God; but if we love one another, God lives in us and His love is made complete in us. We know that we live in Him and He in us, because He has given us of His Spirit. And we have seen and testify that the Father has sent His Son to be the Savior of the world.

1 John 4:7-14 NIV

If I speak in the tongues of men and of angels, but have not love, I am only a resounding gong or a clanging cymbal. If I have the gift of prophecy and can fathom all mysteries and all knowledge, and if I have a faith that can move mountains, but have not love, I am nothing.

If I give all I possess to the poor and surrender my body to the flames, but have not love, I gain nothing. Love is patient, love is kind. It does not envy, it does not boast, it is not proud. It is not rude, it is not self-seeking, it is not easily angered, it keeps no record of wrongs. Love does not delight in evil but rejoices with the truth. It always protects, always trusts, always hopes, always perseveres.

Love never fails. But where there are prophecies, they will cease; where there are tongues, they will be stilled; where there is knowledge, it will pass away. For we know in part and we prophesy in part, but when perfection comes, the imperfect disappears.

When I was a child, I talked like a child, I thought like a child, I reasoned like a child. When I became a man, I put childish ways behind me. Now we see but a poor reflection as in a mirror; then we shall see face to face. Now I know in part; then I shall know fully, even as I am fully known. And now these three remain: faith, hope and love. But the greatest of these is love.

1 Corinthians Chapter 13 NIV

For we are God's workmanship, created in Christ Jesus to do good works, which God prepared in advance for us to do.

Ephesians 2:10 NIV

This is My commandment, that ye love one another, as I have loved you.

John 15:12

He will love you and bless you and increase your numbers. He will bless the fruit of your womb, the crops of your land – your grain, new wine and oil – the calves of your herds and the lambs of your flocks in the land that He swore to your forefathers to give you. You will be blessed more than any other people; none of your men or women will be childless, nor any of your livestock without young.

Deuteronomy 7:13-14 NIV

A Valentine's Day Prayer

Dear Lord,

Please help us to show our animal companions and all animals everywhere the perfect love of God. For we know that God is love (I John 4:7-8). We pray that You'll help us to not only love in word, but in deed and truth according to I John 3:18. We say unto You, Lord, I love the Lord because He hath heard my voice and my supplications (Psalm 116:1). Amen.

Janis Nedelec and her cat, Maui

A cat's love is a projection of God's love for you, because it is completely genuine and unconditional.

Janis Nedelec

Celebrating Music With Your Pet

Hark! Tis the voice of angels
Borne in a song to me,
Over the fields of glory,
Over the jasper sea!

W. H. Doane

Cats Protection, the UK's oldest and largest feline welfare charity, recently released statistics that show that cats have a soft spot for music. They found that 56% liked classical music, closely followed by pop and rock at 42%, and 14% liked easy listening.

Two recent studies have shown that the type of music they are hearing can affect the behavior of dogs. When a team of researchers led by Deborah Wells, an animal behaviorist employed by Queens University in Belfast, Northern Ireland, exposed 50 dogs in an animal shelter to Vivaldis, Greigs Morning and other classical pieces, the dogs became calm and laid down.

When the researchers played music by Metallica and other heavy metal bands, the dogs became agitated and began barking. Pop music and radio talk shows seemed to have little effect.

A similar research project conducted at the Rehoming Center of the National Canine Defense League in Evesham, England yielded comparable results.

"It is well established that music can influence our moods," said Wells. "Dogs may be as discerning as humans when it comes to music."

Music and singing are definitely Biblical. Psalm 100:2 says serve the Lord with gladness; come before His presence with singing.

Make a joyful noise unto the Lord, all the earth:
make a loud noise, and rejoice, and sing praise.
Sing unto the Lord with the harp; with the harp,
and the voice of a psalm. With trumpets and sound of
cornet make a joyful noise before the Lord, the King.

Psalm 98:4-6

Pete and Niki Shanahan

I know all my cats like music. My cat, Joey, likes classical music and Lukie does, too. They also like soft rock and swing music. Leaving soft music on the radio is a good way to help them to relax when you're away from home. They like it when I put on a children's Bible songs CD. We've also found that when we are traveling with the cats, they are calmer for the ride when we put on children's Bible songs.

The Singing Robin

There's a story dated around 1874 about a robin that made himself at home in a woman's dining room. He would come to the window and tap it at breakfast time. When he came in, he shared her oatmeal porridge with her, seated himself on the edge of the cup and picked out such grains as caught his fancy. When he was finished eating, he sat on the back of her chair and sang. This story is taken from Rev. J. G. Wood's *Man and Beast: Here and Hereafter.*

Let's return to John Wesley's journal where we'll read a couple of stories about Wesley and animals. His love for animals really shows through in his personal journal writings.

John Wesley Finds the Horses Enjoy Their Singing

Monday, July 3. I rode to Coolylough (where was the quarterly meeting) and preached at eleven in the evening. While we were singing, I was surprised to see the horses from all parts of the ground gathering about us. Is it true then that horses, as well as lions and tigers have an ear for music?

John Wesley Experiments with Lions

Monday, December 31. I thought it would be worthwhile to make an odd experiment. Remembering how surprisingly fond of music the lion at Edinburgh was, I was determined to see whether this was the case with all animals of the same kind. I accordingly went to the Tower with one who plays on the German flute. He began playing near four or five lions; only one of these (the rest not seeming to regard it at all) rose up, came to the front of his den, and seemed to be all attention.

Meantime, a tiger in the same den started up, leaped over the lion's back, turned and ran under his belly, leaped over him again, and so to and fro incessantly. Can we account for this by any principle of mechanism? Can we account for it at all?

Bible Readings

Praise the Lord with harp; sing unto Him with the psaltery and an instrument of ten strings. Sing unto Him a new song; play skillfully with a loud noise.

Psalm 33:2-3

All the earth bows down to You; they sing praise to You, they sing praise to Your name.

Psalm 66:4 NIV

Speaking to yourselves in psalms and hymns and spiritual songs, singing and making melody in your heart to the Lord. Giving thanks always for all things unto God and the Father in the Name of our Lord Jesus Christ.

Ephesians 5:19-20

You'll see several instruments mentioned by King David which were used to praise God in these verses.

Praise ye the Lord. Praise God in His sanctuary: praise Him in the firmament of His power. Praise Him for His mighty acts: praise Him according to His excellent greatness. Praise Him with the sound of the trumpet: praise Him with the psaltery and harp. Praise Him with the timbrel and dance: praise Him with stringed instruments and organs. Praise Him upon the loud cymbals: praise Him upon the high sounding cymbals. Let every thing that hath breath praise the Lord. Praise ye the Lord.

Psalm Chapter 150

Prayer While Singing

Dear Lord,

We are happy to sing unto You, to play instruments and extol the glories of Thy name. We sing praises to our God, we sing praises to our King just as in Mark 14:26 when they sang a hymn and went out to the Mount of Olives. Singing and music surely brings us joy, and sends up a sweet sound of praise unto You. I will sing with the spirit, and I will sing with the understanding (I Corinthians 14:15). Amen.

It is good to praise the Lord
and make music to Your Name, O Most High.

Psalm 92:1 NIV

Animal Companion Dedication

The smallest feline is a masterpiece.

Leonardo Da Vinci

Joey Shanahan

The Lord has generously blessed us with our beautiful animal companions. Every good thing comes from above. When parents dedicate their babies to the Lord, they are saying thank you for God's beautiful treasures bestowed unto them. They are agreeing to bring the child up in the ways of the Lord, and to honor Him. We can also dedicate our furry babies at any age to the Lord, and thank Him for our priceless blessings. We commit our animal family to the Lord for His tender mercies, divine protection, good health, safety, and soundness of mind.

For song suggestions, see the Bibliography section.

Our furry family members give back more than they receive from us. This was never so true as in this next story.

Feline Saves Couple From Burning House

Duchess, a 6-year-old black and white domestic shorthaired cat who lives in Lillian, Texas, is the latest inductee to the Texas Animal Hall of Fame. Jason and

Jill were asleep in their mobile home about 1:30 a.m. one November when Duchess' knocking on their bedroom door woke them. "She was practically banging down the door," said Jason, who works in Mansfield's parks and recreation department. They opened the door to find their home on fire. "The smoke alarm went off about two minutes after Duchess," Jason said.

"The firemen said if they had gotten there a few minutes later, everything would have blown up." News of Duchess' heroism spread through word of mouth until it reached Dr. Ron Sanders of Park Row Animal Hospital in Arlington. Sanders nominated Duchess for the award, which was instituted in 1984 by the Texas Veterinary Medical Association.

In the book of Exodus Moses wrote about how the animals were included in God's law that there would be no work on the seventh day, because they are part of and included in the household!

Six days you shall labor and do all your work, but the seventh day is a Sabbath to the Lord your God. On it you shall not do any work, neither you, nor your son or daughter, nor your manservant or maidservant, nor your animals, nor the alien within your gates.

Exodus 20:9-10 NIV

Anoint With Oil

Prayer For Dedication Of Your Pet

O Creator of all creatures and giver of life, we are so grateful for this little one. We ask in the Name of Jesus that the Holy Spirit be with [pet's name] parents as they care for their beloved animal companion. Help them to seek out your Word on all matters concerning their family. Lord grant the parents the desire to be as loving to this creature as You would want them to be. O precious Father we especially pray for [name] blessings and well being. We ask that Your heavenly angels would watch over [name]. Let [him/her] receive blessings and keep [him/her] in Thy tender loving care. Bless [name] with a very long, healthy, happy life for the Glory of God. Amen.

Bible Readings

Now I commit you to God and to the Word of His grace, which can build you up and give you an inheritance among all those who are sanctified.

Acts 20:32 NIV

The Lord bless thee, and keep thee: The Lord make His face shine upon thee, and be gracious unto thee: The Lord lift up His countenance upon thee, and give thee peace.

Numbers 6:24-26

For God so loved the world, that He gave His only begotten Son, that whosoever believeth in Him should not perish, but have everlasting life.

John 3:16

I will praise Thee; for I am fearfully and wonderfully made: marvellous are Thy works; and that my soul knoweth right well.

Psalm 139:14

My little dog – a heartbeat at my feet.

Edith Wharton

This Is My Father's World

This is My Father's world,
And to my listening ears,
All nature sings and round me rings
The music of the spheres.
This is My Father's world,
I rest me in the thought
Of rocks and trees, of skies and seas
His hand the wonders wrought.

This is My Father's world,
The birds their carols raise,
The morning light, the lily white,
Declare their Maker's praise.
This is My Father's world,
He shines in all that's fair;
In the rustling grass I hear Him pass,
He speaks to me everywhere.

This is My Father's world,
O let me never forget
That though the wrong seems oft so strong,
God is the ruler yet.
This is My Father's world;
The battle is not done,
Jesus who died shall be satisfied,
And earth and heaven be one.

Maltbie D. Babcock, 1858-1901
– From the Hymn "This Is My Father's World"

Pete and Niki

A merry heart doeth good like a medicine:
but a broken spirit drieth the bones.

Proverbs 17:22

Lukie and Jack

Chapter 7

Memorial Service

Then shall the dust return to the earth as it was,
and the spirit shall return unto God who gave it.

Ecclesiastes 12:7

A memorial service can be done at any time, not just at the time of your beloved animal companion's passing. There are many ways to remember your beloved animal companion. When shopping, the infant sections are a good place to look for such items. Special photos in lovely frames are comforting to have around you. I bought a large collage frame that has the word "baby" on it and filled it with photos of my beloved cat, Pete. I mixed the photos up so that most of them are just Pete, and others are one with Mom, one with Dad and one with his brother, Lukie. In fact, after I did Pete's collage, I liked it so much that I did one for Lukie, too.

You don't have to wait until they go to heaven to celebrate their life! I made their own special photo albums and again, the baby sections work out good because you can find lovely photo albums with Noah's ark and other animals on them.

I also bought a white porcelain cross container which I used to store locks of Pete's hair, whiskers, his nails and his ID tag. I used to save little locks of his hair when it came off, and I would put it in an envelope for the day when we would have to temporarily part.

I recommend that you read my book called *There Is Eternal Life For Animals.* It will bring you great comfort as you study the scriptures, which reveal that all animals go to heaven. Your beloved animal companion's are not only in your past – they are in your future!

Blessed are they that mourn: for they shall be comforted.

Matthew 5:4

… For I will turn their mourning into joy, and will comfort them, and make them rejoice from their sorrow.

Jeremiah 31:13

The Memorial Service

We are confident, I say, and willing rather
to be absent from the body,
and to be present with the Lord.

II Corinthians 5:8

You can include anything personal you may wish to say. For song suggestions, see the Bibliography section.

Prayer In A Memorial Service

Dear Lord,

We commit into Your hands this day Your loving creature, [name]. We ask that [name's] joy would be full in [his/her] new home in heaven. Please reunite us with [name] when we get to heaven ourselves, and bless us with an eternity together. Thank you for the life of this beautiful animal. Thank you for the privilege of enjoying so many months and years of friendship and companionship with Your dear creature. In Jesus' name we pray. Amen.

Bible Readings

God Giving Life

And God said, "Let the land produce living creatures according to their kinds: livestock, creatures that move along the ground, and wild animals, each according to its kind." And it was so. God made the wild animals according to their kinds, the livestock according to their kinds, and all the creatures that move along the ground according to their kinds. And God saw that it was good.

Genesis 1:24-25 NIV

God's Blessing In Life

The Lord is my shepherd; I shall not want. He maketh me to lie down in green pastures: He leadeth me beside the still waters. He restoreth my soul: He leadeth me in the paths of righteousness for His Name's sake. Yea, though I walk through the valley of the shadow of death, I will fear no evil: for Thou art with me; Thy rod and Thy staff they comfort me. Thou preparest a table before me in the presence of mine enemies: Thou anointest my head with oil; my cup runneth over. Surely goodness and mercy shall follow me all the days of my life: and I will dwell in the house of the Lord for ever.

Psalm Chapter 23

The Lord Comforts Us

The Lord is close to the brokenhearted and saves those who are crushed in spirit. A righteous man may have many troubles, but the Lord delivers him from them all.

Psalm 34:18-19 NIV

Jesus Made Eternal Life Possible

For God so loved the world, that He gave His only begotten Son, that whosoever believeth in Him should not perish, but have everlasting life.

John 3:16

Jesus said to her, "I am the resurrection and the life. He who believes in Me will live, even though he dies; and whoever lives and believes in Me will never die. Do you believe this?"

John 11:25-26 NIV

Let not your heart be troubled: ye believe in God, believe also in Me. In My Father's house are many mansions: if it were not so, I would have told you. I go to prepare a place for you. And if I go and prepare a place for you, I will come again, and receive you unto Myself; that where I am, there ye may be also. And whither I go ye know, and the way ye know. Thomas saith unto Him, Lord, we know not whither Thou goest; and how can we know the way? Jesus saith unto him, I am the Way, the Truth, and the Life: no man cometh unto the Father, but by Me.

John 14:1-6

For since by man came death, by man came also the resurrection of the dead. For as in Adam all die, even so in Christ shall all be made alive.

I Corinthians 15:21-22

The Resurrection of Christ

Now, brothers, I want to remind you of the gospel I preached to you, which you received and on which you have taken your stand. By this gospel you are saved, if you hold firmly to the word I preached to you. Otherwise, you have believed in vain.

For what I received I passed on to you as of first importance: that Christ died for our sins according to the Scriptures, that He was buried, that He was raised on the third day according to the Scriptures, and that He appeared to Peter, and then to the Twelve. After that, He appeared to more than five hundred of the brothers at the same time, most of whom are still living, though some have fallen asleep. Then He appeared to James, then to all the apostles, and last of all He appeared to me also, as to one abnormally born. For I am the least of the apostles and do not even deserve to be called an apostle, because I persecuted the church of God. But by the grace of God I am what I am, and His grace to me was not without effect. No, I worked harder than all of them – yet not I, but the grace of God that was with me. Whether, then, it was I or they, this is what we preach, and this is what you believed.

I Corinthians 15:1-11 NIV

God Preserves Man and Animals

Thy righteousness is like the great mountains; Thy judgments are a great deep: O Lord, Thou preservest man and beast.

Psalm 36:6

Thou, even Thou, art Lord alone; Thou hast made heaven, the heaven of heavens, with all their host, the earth, and all things that are therein, the seas, and all that is therein, and Thou preservest them all; and the host of heaven worshippeth Thee.

Nehemiah 9:6

The Resurrection Of The Animals With Us

For I reckon that the sufferings of this present time are not worthy to be compared with the glory which shall be revealed in us. For the earnest expectation of the creature waiteth for the manifestation of the sons of God. For the creature was made subject to vanity, not willingly, but by reason of him who hath subjected the same in hope, Because the creature itself also shall be delivered from the bondage of corruption into the glorious liberty of the children of God. For we know that the whole creation groaneth and travaileth in pain together until now. And not only they, but ourselves also, which have the firstfruits of the Spirit, even we ourselves groan within ourselves, waiting for the adoption, to wit, the redemption of our body. For we are saved by hope: but hope that is seen is not hope: for what a man seeth, why doth he yet hope for? But if we hope for that we see not, then do we with patience wait for it.

Romans 8:18-25

The Lord hath made bare His holy arm in the eyes of all the nations; and all the ends of the earth shall see the salvation of our God.

Isaiah 52:10

Then shall the dust return to the earth as it was, and the spirit shall return unto God who gave it.

Ecclesiastes 12:7

The Resurrection of the Dead

But if it is preached that Christ has been raised from the dead, how can some of you say that there is no resurrection of the dead? If there is no resurrection of the dead, then not even Christ has been raised. And if Christ has not been raised, our preaching is useless and so is your faith.

More than that, we are then found to be false witnesses about God, for we have testified about God that He raised Christ from the dead. But He did not raise Him if in fact the dead are not raised. For if the dead are not raised, then Christ has not been raised either. And if Christ has not been raised, your faith is futile; you are still in your sins. Then those also who have fallen asleep in Christ are lost. If only for this life we have hope in Christ, we are to be pitied more than all men.

But Christ has indeed been raised from the dead, the firstfruits of those who have fallen asleep. For since death came through a man, the resurrection of the dead comes also through a man. For as in Adam all die, so in Christ all will be made alive. But each in his own turn: Christ, the firstfruits; then, when He comes, those who belong to Him. Then the end will come, when He hands over the kingdom to God the Father after He has destroyed all dominion, authority and power. For He must reign until He has put all His enemies under His feet. The last enemy to be destroyed is death. For He "has put everything under His feet."

Now when it says that "everything" has been put under Him, it is clear that this does not include God Himself, who put everything under Christ. When He has done this, then the Son Himself will be made subject to Him who put everything under Him, so that God may be all in all.

I Corinthians 15:12-28 NIV

Is your beloved animal companion still alive? Yes! As you read the next scriptures, note that it says, "If there is a natural body, there is also a spiritual body." The Apostle Paul is speaking about the bodies of mankind and the bodies of animals!

The Resurrection Body

But someone may ask, "How are the dead raised? With what kind of body will they come?" How foolish! What you sow does not come to life unless it dies. When you sow, you do not plant the body that will be, but just a seed, perhaps of wheat or of something else. But God gives it a body as He has determined, and to each kind of seed He gives its own body.

All flesh is not the same: **Men have one kind of flesh, animals have another, birds another and fish another.** There are also heavenly bodies and there are earthly bodies; but the splendor of the heavenly bodies is one kind, and the splendor of the earthly bodies is another. The sun has one kind of splendor, the moon another and the stars another; and star differs from star in splendor.

So will it be with the resurrection of the dead. The body that is sown is perishable, it is raised imperishable; it is sown in dishonor, it is raised in glory; it is sown in weakness, it is raised in power; **it is sown a natural body, it is raised a spiritual body.**

If there is a natural body, there is also a spiritual body. So it is written: "The first man Adam became a living being;" the last Adam, a lifegiving spirit. The spiritual did not come first, but the natural, and after that the spiritual. The first man was of the dust of the earth, the second man from heaven. As was the earthly man, so are those who are of the earth; and as is the man from heaven, so also are those who are of heaven. And just as we have borne the likeness of the earthly man, so shall we bear the likeness of the man from heaven. I declare to you, brothers, that flesh and blood cannot inherit the kingdom of God, nor does the perishable inherit the imperishable.

Listen, I tell you a mystery: We will not all sleep, but we will all be changed – in a flash, in the twinkling of an eye, at the last trumpet. For the trumpet will sound, the dead will be raised imperishable, and we will be changed. For the perishable must clothe itself with the imperishable, and the mortal with immortality.

When the perishable has been clothed with the imperishable, and the mortal with immortality, then the saying that is written will come true: "Death has been swallowed up in victory." "Where, O death, is your victory? Where, O death, is your sting?" The sting of death is sin, and the power of sin is the law. But thanks be to God! He gives us the victory through our Lord Jesus Christ.

I Corinthians 15:35-57 NIV

The Future Told In The Book Of Revelation

And every creature which is in heaven, and on the earth, and under the earth and such as are in the sea, and all that are in them, heard I saying, Blessing, and honour, and glory, and power be unto Him that sitteth upon the throne, and unto the Lamb for ever and ever.

Revelation 5:13

And I saw an angel standing in the sun; and he cried with a loud voice, saying to all the fowls that fly in the midst of heaven, Come and gather yourselves together unto the supper of the great God.

Revelation 19:17

Jesus Will Dry Our Tears

And I heard a loud voice from the throne saying, "Now the dwelling of God is with men, and He will live with them. They will be His people, and God Himself will be with them and be their God. He will wipe every tear from their eyes. There will be no more death or mourning or crying or pain, for the old order of things has passed away."

Revelation 21:3-4 NIV

There is no death!
What seems so is transition:
This life of mortal breath
Is but a suburb of the life elysian,
Whose portal we call death.

Longfellow

Joining Our Animal Companions
In Heaven Someday

If you are not sure that you are ready to go to heaven, you can commit your life to Jesus Christ today. Also, by doing so you will be able to spend eternity with your beloved pet!

A commitment to Christ requires a step of faith, an acceptance of the sacrifice, which He made for you. In dying on the Cross for us Jesus has washed our sins clean with His blood.

Bible Readings

If we confess our sins, He is faithful and just to forgive us our sins, and cleanse us from all unrighteousness.

I John 1:9

That if you confess with your mouth, "Jesus is Lord," and believe in your heart that God raised Him from the dead, you will be saved. For it is with your heart that you believe and are justified, and it is with your mouth that you confess and are saved.

Romans 10:9-10 NIV

Therefore being justified by faith, we have peace with God through our Lord Jesus Christ.

Romans 5:1

If you are ready to make that commitment, and if you want to say "Yes" to Jesus then say the following prayer out loud:

Prayer For Salvation

Dear Jesus. Thank you for the sacrifice You made for me. I am sorry for my past sins and will try my best not to repeat them. I ask Your help to keep this pledge. I know I am not worthy but I willingly accept You as my Lord and Savior, and I thank You for Your blessing over my family and me. Please make me ready today to make heaven my eternal home. Amen.

Bibliography

There Is Eternal Life For Animals, Niki Behrikis Shanahan, Pete Publishing, 2002

Healing The Sick, T. L. Osborn, Harrison House, 1992

King James Version, B. B. Kirkbride Bible Co., Inc., 1964

New International Version, referred to as NIV, Zondervan Bible Publishers, 1978

Man and Beast: Here and Hereafter, Rev. J. G. Wood, George Routledge and Sons, 1874

Petland, Rev. J. G. Wood, Longman's, Green, and Company, 1890

Miracles, Greater Miracles, R. W. Schambach, 2003

Hymns of Glorious Praise, Gospel Publishing House, 1969
> *Hymn references:*
> I Sing The Mighty Power Of God, Isaac Watts
> Amazing Grace, John Newton
> All Creatures Of Our God and King, Saint Francis of Assisi
> This Is My Father's World, Maltbie D. Babcock

There Is Eternal Life For Animals
A Book Based On Bible Scripture
By Niki Behrikis Shanahan

There Is Eternal Life For Animals takes you through the Bible and proves through the scriptures that God has made provision for all the animals to go to heaven. It covers:

- God's relationship with the animals.
- The current life of the animal kingdom.
- The future life of the animals and their restoration.
- What animals are currently in heaven?
- The topic of whether animals have souls and spirits.
- Includes numerous Bible scriptures, opinions and commentaries from Bible Theologians, visions, stories, near-death experiences of children, and personal experiences.
- Reviews many of the original Greek and Hebrew words and their translations.
- Praying for animals.

I hope that this book has been beneficial to you and your beloved animal companions. If you would like to share any stories of healing or other answered prayer with us, we'd love to hear from you – please contact the author at the website or address below. We'd like to know if this book has helped you!

You may order additional copies of:
Animal Prayer Guide
or
There Is Eternal Life For Animals
By visiting us at www.eternalanimals.com
or
Contact the publisher at the following address:

Niki Behrikis Shanahan
Pete Publishing
P. O. Box 282
Tyngsborough, MA 01879

We welcome you to visit us at:
http://www.eternalanimals.com

Our website is dedicated to animals and pets with a focus on animal afterlife from a Christian perspective, prayer for pets, and animal appreciation. You'll find articles, stories, news, health and wellness information, photos, and other resources. We welcome prayer requests for animals.

God Bless You And Your Family!